THE DEVILS *of* EDEN

Joseph Andrew Holsworth

THE DEVILS OF EDEN

A Veteran's Story of Contemporary War

By

Joseph Andrew Holsworth

For the People of Afghanistan.

PROLOGUE

In my four years as a paratrooper, I saw my brothers die in many countries. The following narrative is based on my four months in the Paktia Province along the border of Eastern Afghanistan and Western Pakistan. I wrote this story under the guise of a mild intoxication in 2011.

I grew up in violence. Not in my home, but in school, on the team, in scouts, and in every blockbuster extravaganza of the 80's and 90's. We all did. America loves the gunslinger. From Robocop to John McClain, or John Rambo for that matter, take your pick. The heroes from my generation were men of blood. It started when I was a kid. Kindergarten Cop was the family comedy of my childhood. We had a substitute teacher show it to us in the second grade for Christ's sake. Even Mormons saw the fucking movie; it was in every middle-class family's VHS collection. And what a family oriented story it was. Beginning with Schwarzenegger blasting his way through street junkies and ending with him shooting the drug dealing ex-husband of the teacher he starts fucking while working undercover. Arnold's sex addict partner even clubs the bastard's mother with a baseball bat. Happy, happy, happy, the end.

I couldn't wait to be that hero with a smoking gun. I played cowboys and Indians, capture the flag, and dodge ball as a kid; and I kicked ass at them all. And for most that shit's enough. Most will just play high school football, lift some weights, get into a few fights, and that's all they need – they feel they've fit the mold of the idealized American male image at that point. These individuals are the partially conditioned. If they had been fully conditioned they would have been like me. They'd be a bit unsure of themselves, they'd need to do more, something that even less men would participate in, like say, going to war. By the time I got to high school, American mass media had me feeling like I was a little bitch, like I needed to be kicking ass and waving that flag. You can just play ball. America loves its athletes, nobody questions their manhood; but that shit was no good for me: I was too short for basketball, I wasn't big enough for football, and I couldn't hit a curveball, so the blue-collar badass option of American Soldier seemed the only salvation for my virility. Before I wanted to kill for my country, my socially constructed identity made me need to kill for my country. I actually worried that I might not get my chance. While I watched the towers burn from our high school cafeteria big screen, I remember feeling relief while everybody else felt sadness and fear. I thought only about how I'd have my war.

The few men who were in charge of everything during my late teen years had the wherewithal to manipulate a generation that had been raised to be their pawns since we were shat out of our mothers' wombs. I was dressed as a gun-slinging cowboy before I could walk, a sailor before I could talk. I had my first BB gun when I was five. At eight I got my first rifle, during which time I had already been conditioned to succumb to the symbolic strength of hierarchy and uniformity through family, religion, school, organized sports, and scouts. Especially fucking scouts, with their mini little Gestapo uniforms, and their badges and bullshit. Scouts are perfect for breeding soldiers, getting them used to attempting unreasonable and unfulfilling goals for the reward of a small piece of cloth on a pin. But that shit works like a charm, at least it did on me. By the time I was eighteen, I couldn't wait to strap on the real deal — give me a gun, a pair of boots, and a fucking parachute.

Now I've had somebody to fight, and I've had my war. It didn't make me a man, not even in the bullshit way that America sells its image of man. It gave age to my years, without adding wisdom. I am none the wiser for it. And none the better. And you won't be by reading it. By formerly participating in war, and now by writing about it, I understand quite little in regard to its glories, merits, and justifications. I don't claim to hold an omniscient understanding of the nature of human warfare, nor our curious gravitation toward it. I have but experienced a humble chapter of its savage tale and wish to transpire those happenings to you as affectively as I can. What I write now, I write under the knowledge and understanding eight years of separation from that detestable occupation has afforded me. My actions, and the actions of the soldiers who were with me in 2003, were not the actions of the person depicting them to you today. I cannot be the same soldier that you will read about. I can emulate the attitudes and emotions with only as much truth as my own guilt and anxiety can afford. I stress that a hyperbole of character is dismally unnecessary. The men whose names you will remember are as closely related to their physical selves as is possible through literary adaptation.

This story is not for my brother's in arms, or my fellow Americans. It is not for the Airborne Ranger in the sky. It's not for mom, dad, God, or country. It is not my confession, it's just one of many accounts. If you were born on or around the year 1984, the content of this story could have, with a few different decisions, been the realities of your unrest. If you're much older than that, the following can be understood as an allegorical consequence of an American culture that my generation had no part in fostering.

If you are much younger, just remember, as I grew up Arnold Schwarzenegger was still just the Terminator. Lauren Hill hadn't told white people to stop buying her records yet. Mel Gibson was too busy as a lethal weapon to be drunkenly spewing anti-Semitic remarks at police officers. Police officers were still shooting all kinds of Black people in Los Angeles, though. Los Angeles had found a neo-Jordan from Philly named Kobe. Our president's fuck ups had to do with where he put his dick. People went on vacations every year. Vietnam was kind of being forgotten about. Genocides were quietly ignored. And Y2K and shit like that caused legitimate concern. So that's about where the children of the 1980's were. While I bitch, I had it pretty well.

For myself, and the vast majority of men with

whom I served, the atrocities in which we took part were so unthinkable that it was at first difficult to put into context with the backdrop of our sheltered middle class upbringings. It became rather apparent to me upon observation that the intrepidity of the modern day warrior seemed to be most prevalent in those whom had never expressed the virtues they so passionately wish to exercise.

I was all about it. Fighting, war, all that bullshit. I didn't grow up in the ghetto, and my dad never hit me, but I wanted to kill. I wanted to kill in that fucked up way that they want a certain percentage of young men to want to kill—behind the stars, stripes, and democracy of American liberalism. They built us to fight behind that cause. They built us for this war. You older folks had John Wayne, a bit younger and you had John Rambo. It was the same shit for us. They sold us that the notion to be a man was supreme. And that to be a patriot is to be the best of those men. And there was no better way to prove one's patriotism than to kill for your country. The image seen a thousand times over in old WWII and 'Nam movies of the lowly veteran hunkered over a bottle of cheap Scotch, boo-hooing about the youth he gave up for Uncle Sam was appealing somehow. I wanted to be that poor bastard when I grew up. It was a sick kind of martyrdom that took me to Afghanistan, the plague of a nation after September 11, 2001. I was among the most susceptible.

PART I

GOD LOVES THE INFANTRY

The explosive one.

When one considers how much the energy of young men needs to explode, one is not surprised to see them decide so unsubtly and so unselectively for this or that cause: what thrills them is the sight of the zeal surrounding a cause and, so to speak, the sight of the burning match — and not the cause itself. The subtler seducers therefore know how to create in them the expectation of an explosion and to disregard justifying their cause: reasons are not the way to win over these power kegs!

~Friedrich Nietzsche

I want to be an Airborne Ranger…
Live the life of sex and danger…
Airborne Ranger…
Sex and danger.

~Army Infantry Cadence

JOSEPH AND THE MULTI-CULORED BUS

We rode on giant tour busses with rainbowed sides and matching splatter swirled seats. They had two bathrooms and tiny television sets hanging over our heads. There were sleepers, talkers, and readers. Nobody watched the televisions. I couldn't tell you what they showed. The bus was large enough to hold two stories, but it only had one. There were enough open seats that I didn't have to sit next to anyone. I sat in about the middle, on the passenger side, against the window. The scenery whisked by, one place after the other. The landscape, housing, towns, the people—commuting, gardening. As each scene passed by, the blur of the last hazed into the present. When looking out a window of a moving vehicle, you see things in the same manner that you experience them in life. You never see one scene completely independent of influence from the passing scenes, you're simply moving too fast. You cannot completely focus on any one thing: everything is blended with the influence of the past and the anticipation of the future, and so it is with life.

Thirty newly trained paratroopers were on this North Carolina bound passenger vehicle. As was customary every month, the fresh graduates of Army airborne school from Fort Benning, Georgia, home of the infantry, were transported north to Fort Bragg to fill the ranks of the 82nd Airborne Division and its supporting units. It was a Sunday. George W. Bush was president. The United States suffered its largest attack about a year ago and the nation was at war.

War was never far from the paratroopers' minds. The thought hung like dreams of the Olympics for world-class athletes. World-class warriors were created at Fort Benning. But they were born in the midst of the same atmosphere that surrounds the common civilian. The men on that bus were not afraid of war. Not afraid to die. Few possessed a blind patriotism that extended so far as to render the paratrooper impartial to his time of death. For the men on that bus it was a matter of risk versus reward. The reward of experiencing battle and returning home a veteran was well worth the risk of death and dismemberment, whereas the rewards of not going to war was, for these men, not worth the risk of being a candy ass.

It's often called a brotherhood, although I don't care for the term. That famous HBO series brought it to the living rooms of all those people with the same curiosity as the men on that bus, but without the gumption, or perhaps the carelessness, to materialize it into their reality. I guess

2

most of us felt more temporal than the average person, and that's why we were there. Some would see the war, and most of us would come back. Many would return to the desert, and for those poor souls, war would be life. Some would see war and return to live amongst the virgins. Some had this plan, but would be ceased by war, overtaken from the inside. This war ended lives, stories. This war for me was to be but a chapter, albeit a necessary chapter. The lives, the books, of our generation's past had this chapter. Our best men fought, and they were alongside our worst. They returned as citizens, doctors, teachers, gravediggers, cooks, and carpenters. Their chapter would remain unread to most they knew, but it would still be present throughout their entire lives. The men on that bus wanted that chapter. I went to Fort Bragg to appropriate my destiny.

I'd grown up in the city. Portland, Oregon. I was only one of two people from my high school class to join the military. The other one went to cook grits in the Air Force. Portland, Little Beirut, as H.W. designated the city during the first Gulf War. Not a whole lot of soldiers come from there. Nobody thought I would. In high school I was an athlete with barely above average talent. I'd punched about three people in the face before. I smoked pot. I tried to get laid. I listened to Pink Floyd. And my presence in the military was in many ways a reaction to that upbringing. It had been fun, baseball, and blowjobs. Middle-class affords that. I learned less than I should have. I experienced a bit more than most of my peers I suppose, which was to say that I had experienced almost nothing in comparison with a seventeen-year-old living in Southern Sudan. Bits of martyrdom amongst a towering rage of teenage hormones, plus sexual frustration and middle-class angst equals the modern day grunt. Admiration played its role. My grandfather fought in World War II. I never knew the details. It didn't matter. Grandpa was a hero because he killed men under the moral guise of a military uniform.

My joining was unexpected. Both of my parents went to college, even my grandmother did. My aunts and uncles did the same. Our family was fast set to establish itself as upper-middle class, gathering that coveted "American wealth." As an only child without cousins on my uncle's side, I was my family's sole representative. Joining the Airborne Infantry was for them stepping back a couple of generations. Looking upon my grandfather in the backdrop of the rest of my family, I was sure that I had made the right choice.

I didn't know anybody on the bus. Out of the five of us who, after infantry training, went on to airborne school, four of us would be pinned with wings. Due to the army's need for additional mechanized soldiers, two got the high hard one, and got stuck at Fort Benning with the Third Infantry Division, mechanized. Riding in tanks was no life for a grunt. A buddy of mine, Solomon, graduated with a broken foot from the last jump of Airborne School, so I was the lone representative from my infantry class.

Listening to a conversation between two troopers a couple of seats back, I was reminded of how long it had been since I'd watched a ball game. My Mariners kicked ass the year before, second best record ever. Best year to be a fan in franchise history, until the playoffs, first fucking series, out to the Yankees, the fucking Yankees. But none of that shit mattered anymore. The Mariners didn't matter. My friends didn't matter, or my girlfriend, or my family, it was just me. And soon my rifle.

I couldn't understand why those guys even talked. Maybe just to pass time? Were they really trying to get to know each other? Exchanging stories about pussy is one thing, but talking about family? Often I felt like I was the only one ready to go to the war. Even the guys in my infantry class, with their letters home every week, their fucking pictures taped to the inside of their lockers. I thought of them as weaker for their sentimentality. I didn't attempt to reduce my needs and desires in the Buddhist sense of the idea; it was simply that my only need and desire was for a trip to Afghanistan and a kill.

I figured I'd call my dad before I arrived at Bragg. I knew I wouldn't have much time once I was there. I had to call back after no answer on the first call, which is how it always was with my parents. My fathered answered, "Yellow." Even though we're from the city and my Dad has never been on a horse in his life, he thinks he's a cowboy. "Hey it's just me. I'm still on the bus."

"A bus? What are you on a bus for, I thought you were airborne," chuckles followed.

"Yeah well, I uh, I'm just on my way up to Bragg."

"I know, I know, I was just kidding around." My father had to reveal that he was just kidding often.

"What are you guys up to?"

"Oh your mother is just puttering around in her flower garden. We took your Grandmother out to lunch a bit earlier. It's getting dark, so not much else tonight. Well, are you excited?"

"Yeah, I'm still a bit nervous that I'm not going to get assigned to the 82nd though."

"What do you mean? You just got your Airborne wings, that's where you go after that."

"Usually, yeah. But sometimes you end up in some bullshit little support regiment driving a Colonel or something."

"Oh don't get yourself worked up about that. That's where they send the freckly-faced little dweebs that barely make it through. You'll be an 82nd grunt, don't worry about that." My dad never served and had no idea what he was talking about, but his words still comforted me.

"I'd better. I just really need it to work out. Everything else has, but I don't know. I'm sure I'll be good. The chances are small. This is the last thing that's out of my hands though."

"Don't forget that once you get overseas son everything is going to be out of your hands." When my father managed to accidentally instill confidence, he always managed to take it back within seconds.

"Yeah I know, but I'll have a rifle then at least."

"Ha, ha, yeah, that's true, yeah you will. Well it sounds like you're doing well. I'm going to have to talk to you later though son, the new CSI is about to come on and

I have to go get your mother. You should try to get some sleep before you get up there. They'll probably run you around as soon as you get there. "

"Probably. Tell mom I said hi. I'll call you guys in a few days when I find out what unit I'm going to and stuff."

"Alright son, you take care."

"Bye Dad."

I wasn't tired enough to fall asleep and about half the soldiers were still awake and talking quietly in pairs. I thought about basic training. For the first time since graduation, I thought about Private Holster.

PRIVATE HOLSTER

Infantrymen of the US Army are born only at Fort
Benning, Georgia. Private Holster never left. Infantry
classes graduate by company. Four platoons that start with
about sixty men make up the company of potential infantry
graduates. Each platoon has two drill sergeants assigned to
equip each soldier with the skills demanded of an
infantryman in the US Army. Mostly they ensure that at any
given time, every soldier under their command fears that he
is about to be fucked up. The platoon stays together in a
kind of studio configuration. The rectangular room, called a
bay, is divided into unequal thirds. The largest third is in
the middle and consists only of empty space. On each side
of the middle portion is a line of blue tape that runs from
one end of the bay to the other, about ten feet wide on each
side. So one could imagine it as a basketball court, the side-
lines being our space, everything else being the drill
sergeants. Spaced exactly the same distance apart on each

side were fifteen bunks. Two soldiers for fourteen weeks shared a bunk and this space of about ten feet by five feet. The configuration differed only slightly from a jail cell; the space available to the individual was less. The middle portion of the bay belonged to the drill sergeants. At the end of each side there was a single door that lead into the bathroom, or head as it was called. On each side of the head there were five showers, ten toilets and ten sinks in the middle. On the side opposite of where Holster and I resided was a broom closet where the platoon's cleaning products were. Each night, two soldiers performed fireguard, a roaming patrol of the platoon's bay area; one guy at the desk by the door, and the other walking pointlessly around the barracks with a flashlight.

After ten weeks I knew Holster as well as anybody in the platoon, which was to say that I knew where he was from and that he liked movies. Holster's demeanor was tranquil and friendly. He seemed unaffected. I never knew what he was thinking about, and I didn't care. I wasn't there to talk and to hear people's stories. I was there to learn how to kill an enemy. The soldiers who in basic training engaged in unnecessary social activity were in my eyes all the weaker for desiring such trivial human contact. I didn't go to Fort Benning to make friends and form lifelong brotherhoods. I went to learn to kill. I didn't know why Holster went.

Following a four-day training exercise where we slept in half shelters in the field, the platoon was tired and hungry. Holster and I had fireguard, so that longing for a bed had to go unsatisfied for just a bit longer. All I thought about was the next day's training and how after it was over I would be able to get a cool five hours of sleep on that beloved twin bunk. Most soldiers on fireguard talked of life before the army: girls, booze, and drugs. Holster and I just took turns reading field manuals while the other would walk up and down the bay with a flashlight. It's Holster's face that I will always remember, the way it looked when it was still bright with life.

Holding an L shaped flashlight in my left hand while my right thumb paged through the Ranger Handbook, the sound of Holster's boot heels coming in contact with the cold tile got louder. I looked up just as I felt him before me.

"Hey man, I gotta shit, you got this yourself for a few minutes?"

"Got it." That was all I said, that was end of the conversation.

It was three-twenty in the morning when I last looked at my watch. Holster went to the bathroom something like ten minutes before that and I had to take a piss. I figured that instead of the number two that Holster claimed, he was taking what an infantryman refers to as a number three. A piss (#1), a shit (#2), or a jackoff (#3). If he was doing all three, he could easily be another ten minutes, and I couldn't wait. One soldier was to remain in front of the door to the entrance of the bay, opposite the head. If a drill sergeant happened upon the bay and there was no guard in front of the door, it was our ass, then the whole platoon's ass, which meant later it was especially our ass. That blanket party shit you've seen on Full Metal Jacket is no hyperbole. Leaving the desk was a risk but so was pissing my pants. I ran along the blue tape down to the opposite end of the bay.

I assumed Holster was in one of the stalls to my back, and every grunt knows that fireguard is the best time to masturbate with a relatively low risk of being disturbed. If a soldier suspected that he had entered the proximity of a fellow infantryman who was in the midst of a masturbatory session, the infantryman was wont to foil his fellow soldier's plan with the interruption of a proclamation regarding one's shit, or something to a similarly arresting affect. I didn't usually engage in such tomfoolery but given the situation, I gave a simple utterance. "What the fuck Holster? If we get fucked up for this I'm going to rip your fucking dick off." There was no response. "Yeah just keep going motherfucker, might as well finish it out now." Still nothing came, and I began to get frustrated. "Fuck you man." I finished pissing and still no report from Holster. Without washing my hands, I walked out of the head.

No drill sergeant awaited my return with crossed arms and a diabolical grin, and relief washed over me in an awesome wave. Leaving one's post, no matter what the circumstances, could have dire consequences. Twenty more minutes passed and I needed to stretch my legs, I was still all janked up from sleeping on the ground for three nights. It was odd. Holster was not prone to jerking off on guard. I knew that much about him. And I knew that there wasn't a digestive system in the world that could be backed up by that food. Holster was too goddamn regular. Maybe he fell asleep on the shitter or something, it's happened. My curiosity took me from my post once again. This time I walked through the bay slowly, I should have been in a hurry, but my curious anticipation slowed my approach. As I came to the door I whispered, "Holster, you okay in here man, you been in here for like a half hour?" Standing by the row of sinks, the smell of bleach filled my nostrils as an eerie feeling rushed through me at the sight of the legless toilet stalls. There was nothing. "Holster, what the fuck? Where the fuck are you?" There was nowhere else to go, so I walked to the shower. I didn't want to turn on the lights at risk of waking up the entire platoon, so I cut through the darkness with the beam of my L shaped flashlight. The showers were empty, of course the showers were empty, what the fuck would Holster have been doing just standing in the shower fully dressed without the water running? He's not that fucking weird. I was further perplexed. "Holster, where you fucking hiding, what the fuck man? You are going to get our asses in the fucking sling man." By this time, I assumed that Holster was just out of character and was fucking around. I thought he must have been standing on one of the goddamn toilets, just fucking with me. I thought surely at any moment he would jump out from nowhere with the climax of his ruse. So as to try and not wake anybody up, I maintained noise discipline. I gently pushed open the first stall door, then the next. I began to get frustrated and that frustration manifested in an increased amount of force being applied to each new door I came to.

The last one I kicked open, bellowing, "FUCK YOU." I didn't at all consider the noise I must have made. I was astonished that I had come across nothing. I turned off my torch and rested my hands on my hip. I had abandoned my post, I had likely woken up half the platoon, my bunk mate was gone, and if the drill sergeant wasn't waiting for me before, he sure as fuck was after that last kick.

I was perplexed to the point of nausea. I scratched my shaved head with the edge of the bill of my patrol cap. I panned the ground, not looking for Holster, but looking for some sense. I walked out of the head and looked down the bay without the beam of my flashlight. I could see a couple of people sitting part way up in their bunks, but nobody was walking around, and there was not yet any drill instructor at the desk. I turned around and walked a couple of steps back into the head. I had deep in my stomach a peculiar empty sensation that I have not felt since. My head was heavy to one side, my neck stiff, my lip was curled with affliction. All the physical manifestations of my stress and confusion for a moment dissipated when I saw something that I could not recollect ever before seeing. Upon noticing, I marveled at how this sight could have possibly escaped my attention before, but alas, there it was before me like never before. The broom closet door, I had never seen the broad side of that door, it was never closed, it had never in its history of being a door been closed as far the platoon was concerned. I had never even imagined that closet with a door. The broom closet had always stayed open as it was ordered to by the proclamation of Senior

Drill Sergeant Allan. I approached the door. The thought of Holster was still in my mind, but it lingered as a past affliction. I held my flashlight to the door so that in the middle the beam appeared as an illuminated circle which grew fuzzy toward the edges of the light. My opposite hand came to the door handle, putting just enough tension on it, I could tell that it was unlocked. The circle of light waned until my flashlight lens was pressed flush with the door and no more light could escape. For whatever reason I turned off my light. I twisted the knob slowly and gently and pushed the pine barrier upon its silent hinges. As I opened it, I jumped back in a startled haze. I was more astounded that Holster's silhouette remained motionless than I was by his mere presence. "Fuck you Holster, you scared the shit out of me you creepy fucker." I was furious and relieved all at once. A confused feeling for both mind and body, it was like being famished with hunger and having to take a burning shit at the same time.

    I took a deep breath, pulling the collar of my brown t-shirt from my neck. I said with a semblance of relief, "What the fuck dude, what the fuck are you doing in there man?" Holster hadn't even looked at me, I could tell through the darkness that it was him, and that he was facing me, but his head was down, pointed toward me. Why the strange posture, why hadn't he said anything, how hadn't he moved yet? The fury of my panic had certainly aroused a suspicious scene, but Holster had yet to respond to my gestures. I thought of this as I made my way toward him and my thoughts climaxed into a state of astonishing disarray as I made contact with him. I sent him spinning in a circle as if he were rotating perfectly upon an invisible pedestal. The tension of the rope pulled him back the opposite direction. As he spun back around, his face was illuminated by the beam of my L-shaped flashlight. His eyes still opened, his tongue was chewed and hanging from his lips. I saw him one last time.

ALPHA COMPANY

Battalion headquarters had sent a freckle and zit faced kid, about two years my senior, to pick me up from what was referred to at Battalion as Repo, meaning Replacement. I hadn't left in the morning as I had been told I would the day before. It was the next night before I would leave. Aside from a short exchange of me confirming my name, the driver and I said nothing to each other for the ten minute drive from Repo to 3/504 Battalion Headquarters. Replacement assigned me to the 3rd Battalion of the 504th Parachute Infantry Regiment of the 82nd Airborne Division. I was going to the unit that had been dubbed in WWII by the Nazis as "The Devil Brigade;" quite the moniker considering the source, but that's who we were, "The Devils."

Battalion Headquarters looked, to my surprise, very reminiscent of a traditional office building. Grey, long, rectangular, three stories. The perfectly groomed front lawn displayed three poles mounted in a small rock garden of blue, yellow, and white (the Battalion colors), they supported the flags of the United States, the 82nd Airborne Division, and the 504th Parachute Infantry Regiment. All but a few windows on the bottom floor were blackened with darkness. The pickup driver told me to just go inside to the desk, and tell them that I just came from Repo. Between the humvee and the three concrete steps leading up to the Headquarters door, I imagined a parallel universe where at that given moment I chose to bail on the whole fucking plan and just bolted off into the darkness and right out of Fort Bragg to god knows where. I came to the first set of double glass doors. I took a breath and went in.

At the desk there was a Staff Sergeant reading a copy of "Gun Digest" and a Specialist talking to his girlfriend on his cell phone. I gave them my paperwork, and the Staff Sergeant, without expression, told me to walk down the hall and take the second right and have a seat, that the Sergeant Major would be in soon to give his briefing.

The room was empty and the light was off when I walked in. I thought again about Holster. There was enough light from down the hall to illuminate the room plenty to see, so I decided to not disturb things and left the light off and took a seat at the large wooden rectangular table. There was enough light in the room for me to clearly see the large etching of the Battalion crest in the middle of the desk. A flaming saber across a Knight's shield, the words 'Strike Hold' inscribed at the bottom. I sat there with my elbows up and my head in my hands as I stared at my new Battalion crest. Once I left Benning, every moment that went by became more real than the last. I could feel myself getting closer to a big slap in the face. I just didn't know where it was going to come from. I would have nodded off in the darkness had it not been for my nerves that felt like they were stretching like rubber bands around my nuts.

To my relief after just a couple of minutes the Sergeant Major came in, by himself, short as all fuck, all dirty, with cammo all over his face. His battle dress uniform was caked in mud and his boots looked like he had waded through shit. I snapped to parade rest as he walked in. Keeping my head and eyes forward, I examined him from my peripherals. He was much younger than the sergeant majors I saw at Benning, maybe forty. I marveled at the patches on his uniform. He had been to virtually every combat arms school the army had to offer: Ranger, Jumpmaster wings, Halo wings, Pathfinder. He smelled like fresh bark dust on a summer day, and swallowed his tobacco spit. "What's your name paratrooper?"

"Private Harris, Sergeant Major."

"What's your first name private?

"Joseph, Sergeant Major."

"You don't go by Joseph like some kind of faggot, do you paratrooper?" I was caught off guard, I tried my best not to snicker or even pause.

"No Sergeant Major, I go by Joe, Sergeant Major."

"Joe's a good strong name son, ain't never met a faggot who goes by Joe. You know my name Private

Harris?"

"Negative Sergeant Major." It was like the first day of basic, I just got there and I was already fucking up. He took a slow step forward with one foot. Leaning into my face, I could tell he hadn't brushed his teeth since he'd been in the field. "Learn your chain of command paratrooper. How you going to know who to listen to and who to tell to go fuck themselves if you don't know who's who? Roger?" Most Sergeant Majors weren't trying to break balls all that much. They usually had twenty years and were eligible for retirement. They didn't stay in to crush privates. They stayed in because they loved their jobs. This guy was no different.

"Roger that, Sergeant Major." At the moment I didn't know whether or not to laugh. That same situation that everybody has been in with a new boss, do you laugh at what seems to be casual humor and take that chance of being inappropriate, or do you take the risk of being always professional but at the same time frigid? Considering the circumstances of our association, I chose to take the conservative approach. It was hard to recognize his slight smile through the cammo until I saw it drop off his face completely upon my concrete response. "You're going to have to learn how to smile every now and then paratrooper. You won't make it in this business if you don't son." He turned right to business. "You're going to Alpha Company. The best company in my battalion. Probably going to first platoon, get with Sergeant First Class Holliday, he's a big burly black guy, can't miss him." Had I seen more black men in the infantry, I might have though more about that statement. "They'll still be in the field until tomorrow night, but you can get with whoever the Company desk sergeant is and they can set you up with a room. I gotta get back out to the field, where you should be paratrooper. Should have been here two goddamn weeks ago. Too late now. Well, you ready to go to war paratrooper?"

"Airborne Sergeant Major."

"ALL THE WAY PRIVATE."

Behind Battalion Headquarters resided five Company Headquarters buildings. One for Headquarters Company, one for Alpha, one for Bravo, one for Charlie, and one for Delta. The battalion area consisted of six buildings total, within a large rectangular configuration, like a football field. The Battalion Headquarters building being one end zone, the rest of the area dispersed in order and evenly among the respective Companies. As I walked through Battalion I marveled at the uniformity of the buildings. The whole structure was dress right dress, just like they taught us in basic. It was both impressive and intimidating. When I got to Alpha Company Headquarters, I approached with the same apprehension as I had in Battalion. It was the same setup, just a micro version. Instead of a Staff Sergeant and Specialist at a big desk, it was a Sergeant and a Private at a smaller desk. They seemed to know I was coming, but took no more of an interest than they had at Battalion. They knew where I was supposed to go, and assigned me a room. They told me that my roommate would be in the field until the next night, but to just put my stuff in the empty wall locker and to make sure that I was around the company area waiting for them to get back. The key didn't work so they gave me a cot and I slept on that in a squad leader office until six the next morning. They squared away my key situation with some considerable trouble and I spent the next day doing PT by myself and wandering around the Battalion area. It was like an infantry amusement park. Next to the battalion area was a PT area the size of three football fields. There were ropes that went fifty feet up, not like gym class, no knots. There were walls with ropes, and walls without, there were grappling pits, mud pits, dip bars, pull up bars, monkey bars, zip lines, and a mile long track that ran all the way around. I did two laps slowly, the whole time marveling at the exercising units. There were so many individual groups, fire team sized, four or five guys, but at least a hundred of them. It seems like it would be chaotic, but it wasn't, it was like nothing I had seen before. It was like clockwork. I went out to the field at around 0630 and fucked around until about 0930 when the last groups of soldiers cleared the area. Breakfast afterward was a bit better than at Benning. The showers had hot water and my room had a window.

I tried to pass the time with a phone call home, but got nobody on the other end. I called my girlfriend who I was starting to miss now that training was over. I still had some stationary from basic training that I hadn't used of while I was there. I unpacked the contents of my bag into my wall locker, put on my battle duty uniform for the day, and sat down at the desk in my new room to write a letter to my girlfriend, Samantha. I wanted to say something nice, something sweet that would make her miss me, but I didn't have anything. I tried, I wrote a few things and wrinkled up the pages after the first few sentences. We hadn't talked much since I'd left for basic. I wanted her to know that I still thought of her and that I still loved her. I couldn't produce anything, so after an hour I called her back, and when I still didn't get an answer, I left a semi unpleasant message on her voice mail.

Around noon I walked to the closest post-exchange, which is just the Army's version of a convenience store. It had a Taco Bell inside so I got a couple of burritos and walked back to the company area. I had a Ranger handbook that I had bought on the first of the two PX visits we were afforded in basic training. I sat in the company quad and waited for the next four hours with my favorite field manual. At about six individual units from the battalion began to filter in, four, five, six at a time. After their two-week field training exercise, they force marched, by fire team, or in some cases platoon or squad sized elements, ten miles back to the battalion area. I had no idea who or what to look for, except maybe a tall burly black guy like the Sergeant Major said. I kept reading the manual, so as to look like I belonged there, although, my clean uniform and puffy new maroon beret, gave all that away. A tall, good-looking soldier followed by nine others approached me immediately.

Before he said anything, I snapped up to parade rest. "At ease, take it easy. I'm Sergeant Eden, I'm alpha team leader. I think you're my new guy. How long you been here?"

"I just got here today, Sergeant." He nodded and spit a wad of tobacco spit to the side. "Who picked you up?"

"Uh… Private Bernard and a Specialist something. I can't remember, sergeant.

"Oh probably Longley, that shit bag. Anyway man, yeah, I'm sure you were briefed…who briefed you at battalion, Sergeant Major?"

"Roger, sergeant. He was all dirty and wet and still had cammo on his face, sergeant."

"Yeah he's a crazy fucker, you'll get to know him. Still loves the field."

"HOOAH sergeant." He smiled at me and nodded his head slowly. "Calm down with that shit man. I just got out of the field. And besides, there's nobody around man. If Sergeant Holliday is around, then do the private thing, that's the platoon sergeant. But me, I don't give a fuck about all that formality." He spit again and wiped his chin with the back of his hand. "That shit doesn't go for the other squad leaders though man, when you're around them, any E-4 even, just go to parade rest. You're gonna get fucked with about shit like that for a while, just be cool and stay with me and the other guys in Alpha team. Staff Sergeant Reynolds, our squad leader, is the main man you'll have to deal with, and he's not going to fuck with you if you're shit stays tight. Other than that, just listen to what I say and don't bitch, and if you have to bitch, bitch to me first man. Keep with that, you'll be straight." His gaze dropped from my eyes down at my posture. He smiled and chuckled this time as he shook his head. In the midst of his speech I had slipped back into parade rest. "Damn man, I told you, you can calm down with all that shit. Take your hands out from behind your back. You don't need to be at parade rest until I put you there man. Hooah?" I couldn't help my formal posture. I could already tell that Sgt. Eden was a brand of sergeant that was rare to the ranks. He was very nonchalant, and he said 'man' after almost everything.

"Hooah sergeant. When are we supposed to go to Afghanistan sergeant?"

"Anytime in the next couple of weeks. I assume you already processed into battalion or you'd never have known to come here."

"Roger that sergeant." He reached into his lip and hooked out his tobacco with one finger and flung it to the side. "We'll just be cleaning weapons and gear and shit from the field for the next couple of days before the weekend; it'll be a good chance for you to get to know everyone in the platoon, man. I'd take you around Bragg and shit, but you may only be here for a few days. " He smiled, but I knew he was serious.

"Hooah sergeant."

"Yeah, yeah, yeah, yeah, we'll see how fucking hooah you are humping those mountains in Afghanistan man. It sucks you missed this field problem man, could have at least gotten a crash course in some of the basic shit." He looked at me concerned for a moment then shook it off, returning to his casual appearance. "Just listen to everything you can until we take off man. None of us have been there yet, so I don't have shit to tell you except to enjoy yourself before we go and try to get to know as many people as you can. We'll get a case of beer and I'll cover our basic team and squad movements with you this weekend. Do you already have a room, who you with man?"

"Roger sergeant, I'm in a room with Specialist Tolson, sergeant."

"Fucking Tolson? Jeeeesus." His head went back as his smile grew and he rocked back on his heels. "Tolson's cool man, you'll be good, he's bravo team's SAW gunner. Well, go change out of that shit man. I gotta go clean two weeks of dirt off my nuts. Then I'll come by your room, we'll get some food. Probably just going to the dining facility tonight, but that's cool, you'll need to know where that shit's at. Alright man, introduce yourself around to some of the guys you see, everyone on the third floor is in first platoon so...you know get to know 'em man. I'll be by your room in a half hour or so."

"Roger that sergeant. Thirty minutes sergeant." I wasn't trying to be overly formal, but I was excited.

With a grin, Sgt. Eden responded back, "Yeah thirty minutes man."

Meeting sergeant Eden was a breath of fresh air in an otherwise putrid scene.

Walking through the barracks hallway, back to my room, I crossed paths with many members of my new platoon, all caked with grime from head to toe their ruck sacks covered in the same earthy crusting. The only things free of mire were their weapons, still glimmering black. I didn't talk to anyone. Most of them looked at me as I walked by, but nobody said anything. I walked slowly to my room with one thought reverberating in my mind: this is the airborne. I got a good jolt of some of that warrior testosterone that had seemed to fade since infantry school.

Specialist Tolson was already in the room as I returned. Opening the door, there stood a wiry naked paratrooper hopping around on one foot, jungle boots clinging to an ankle. I started to close the door then stopped, when he said in a startled voice, "Hey, who the fuck are you?"

"I'm Private…"

"Oh shit, you're the new guy in first squad. They told me while we were out there that you were moving into my room since Menzo left. What squad are you in?" Tolson had kept taking his pants off, and now stood completely bottomless before me. He tossed his pants into a nearby hamper, took a sigh of relief, and stood there with his arms crossed. It was like he didn't realize that his dick was out.

"First squad, Specialist."

"You don't have to call me Specialist, or stand at parade rest or anything, unless platoon sergeant is around. So you're Sergeant Eden's new guy right?"

I was able to relax. "Looks like it." He finally walked over to his wall locker and put a green army issue towel around his waste.

"Shit, you lucked out, Alpha is where it's at—lucky you're not under Lyons, he's a real cocksucker. He runs Bravo team. I've been his SAW gunner for the last year. Try to stay away from Sergeant Lyons as much as you can, I'm telling you. Be grateful you got Eden, he'll take care of you." He held up his fist and I brought mine up to meet it. "Well, welcome to first platoon Cherry. Have you eaten yet?"

"No. I'm waiting for Sergeant Eden, he's going to come get me and we're going to the D-FAC." Grabbing a shaving kit from inside his girls and guns clad wall locker he said, "Let me get in the shower real quick too and I'll go with you guys." I was relieved by Tolson's demeanor. He seemed happy about having a roommate, rather than pissed that he was again going to have to share with somebody.

After changing out of my BDU's into civilian clothes I waited for Sergeant Eden and Tolson. I was drawn toward Tolson's three stack DVD collection, which at first glance consisted of at least fifty percent pornographic releases. He's got over a hundred, I thought. A sudden knock at the door startled me like a kid with his hand in the cookie jar.

I opened the door to a frothy looking guy in track pants and no shirt, but enough tattoos as to appear fully clothed. I anticipated that this encounter would be less pleasant that my last two.

"Who the fuck are you, and where the fuck is Tolson?"

"I'm…"

"Get the fuck at parade rest. Where the fuck is that piece of shit Tolson at?" As he spoke, he pumped his right index finger back and forth at my face.

With hesitation, I answered. "He went to take a shower."

"How about, he went to go take a shower SERGEANT, you little piece of shit? Now do some fucking pushups."

Having no idea of the rank of the man yelling at me with a hatred that would seem reserved for mortal enemies, I dropped to the floor and began doing pushups as if I were in day one of basic training. "That's right, keep pushing motherfucker. You must be Eden's new cherry. You'll learn who the fuck's who around here, motherfucker. Or you won't fucking survive. Roger?" Standing above me he stepped forward and stepped on my left hand, but he didn't step all the way down. I guess he was just letting me know. Keeping my head and eyes to the front, I answered loudly from the ground, "Roger Sergeant."

"Roger what?"

"Roger, I will learn who is who around here Sergeant."

"Yeah we'll fucking see Cherry. Do flutter kicks." Rolling to my back I slid my hands to the sides of my body, keeping my arms straight and stiff, fingers together and flush, legs out straight, I lifted one leg up, then brought it down while bringing up the other, and repeated the motion continually until he released me from my position. "Get the fuck up. Tell that fucking roommate of yours to power up and hydrate for dinner, I'll be back here to see him after chow, and he'd better fucking be here, or I'm gonna fuck up the both of you. Got it Cherry?" With the last words of his sentence, I thought his finger was going to joust me right through the eyeball.

"Roger Sergeant, tell Tolson to hydrate and be back in the room after chow."

"I didn't ask for a fucking read back Cherry. Just say fucking 'roger', and shut the fuck up, HOOAH?"

"Hooah sergeant."

DINNER AND DRINKS

As another knock followed my encounter with who I could only assume to be the same cock-sucking Sergeant Lyons, I had an anxious hesitation. I knew that I had no choice but to answer the door for whoever waited on the other side. I bit the inside of my lip and turned the brass knob swiftly. Standing before me was a lengthy uniformed soldier who looked to be in his early twenties with a greasy brow, large ears, and an appeased grin between his sunken cheeks.

"You Tolson's new roomie?" I had never heard an accent so Southern in all of my life. I thought at first that it had to be exaggerated. I shook my head and answered, "Roger." His grin immediately grew to a crooked smile. "Well get the fuck out here then Cherry."

What was at first one slightly built blonde haired Specialist named Van Dorn, denoted by his battle duty uniform nametape, quickly exposed itself as a triad of soldiers, each grabbing me and ripping me from my new domicile. As I compliantly stepped through my door, I felt four hands pull me, and out of my peripherals, I could see a man on each side of me, pulling me into the hallway and away from my door. I lunged forward from the force of their pull, and as I looked back I saw the two additional soldiers, clad in battle dress uniform, standing on each side of the door so as to indicate that I had nowhere to go. Van Dorn stood before me like a 20th century dictator. He was grossly unattractive, but the metal crest of his beret shined triumphantly under the florescent hall lights. The other two, whose name-tapes I hadn't seen, began slowly walking in a circle around us. It felt like a street gang musical. The two closed in tighter with every passing rotation until I was finally forced to step forward toward Van Dorn who hadn't moved. With only two feet between us, he closed the gap even tighter with a step forward. I could smell the tobacco in his lip, our noses almost touching. His lackeys circled us like vultures waiting to pick my bones. Van Dorn brought an empty clear bottle to his mouth, spitting into it, droplets of saliva and tobacco dripped down the edge. He looked me up and down with his beady blue eyes. His hooked nose almost speared my forehead. "By the look of that piece a shit on top your head, you in the wrong place Cherry." My beret was all fucked up; it didn't look at all cool and fitted like his did. See, paratroopers wear maroon beret's, instead of the standard patrol cap. But you don't get it after airborne school. You get it when you go to your battalion. I had just gotten mine, and found that they don't come with that coveted badass slant look about them. I put it on new expecting to look like a commando, and instead looked more like a goddamn line chef. That was the piece of shit on top of my head that Van Dorn was referring to. I knew what he meant, but answered, "Negative Specialist, I am Sergeant Eden's guy." My tone was more caustic than I had wanted. Van Dorn's lip curled with distain as my words came out.

"Oh you're Sergeant Eden's guy." The two others had stopped circling Van Dorn and were standing quietly on each side behind him. The shorter of the two, whose name and rank were then visible to me as Specialist Valentine chimed in. His broad face and round head matched his body type as well as his voice. His eyes were wide and green and incapable of holding hostility. He wore an innocence that broke through in a slight smile shining through his authoritative conditioning. Specialist Valentine was as hard as a coffin nail, but his face said he was all act. Van Dorn's countenance on the other hand said that this taunting was his favorite part of the job. His face was still close enough to see my reflection in his eyes. Valentine said with a forced sarcasm, "I thought we were Sergeant Eden's?" Van Dorn smiled exposing yellow teeth peppered with bits of tobacco. "Well I guess not, I guess the Cherry here is Sergeant Eden's guy. Guess I ain't got a job no more boys. Guess none us do. That right Cherry, you taking over my job?"

"Negative Specialist. I met with Sergeant Eden earlier. He informed me that I was to be his new grenadier, Specialist."

"Informed? " Stepping closer, Van Dorn's height allowed him to look down into my eyes, the tip of his nose bumped off mine as he bellowed in my face, "Cherry, you ain't shit. You don't know shit. Sergeant don't tell you shit, he tells me and I let you know, ROGER? You ain't no grenadier Cherry, you ain't no member of my Alpha team, you ain't no paratrooper yet, Cherry. Roger?"

"Roger, Specialist."

"Where are you from Cherry?" Valentine's voice was quick but carried a soothing calmness after Van Dorn's affront.

"Portland, Oregon Specialist, born and bred." The other soldier, whose name-tape I still couldn't read, was enormous, he looked at least 6' 3", 230 pounds, and dumb. I couldn't peg accents, but he was definitely from New York.

"I knew a guy from Portland. Remember that Dorn, that asshole from Charlie Company mortars, got busted at Shughart and Gordon with a fucking bag of weed?" Van Dorn doesn't answer right away, he just smiled and kept leering into my eyes. His grin told me he would kill, fuck, and burn me if he could, in no particular order.

Still in my face, without flinching he answered, "Yeah, I remember that piece of shit, funny fucker." Well how bout it Cherry, you a fucking hippy too? We gonna catch you out in the field with a fucking satchel a dope?"

"Negative Specialist." Valentine took a step to the side, as to break away from the pack. He asked, "You know we're going to Afghanistan in a couple weeks?"

"Roger that Specialist. I specifically requested assignment to this battalion because of that."

"So you're ready then?" Valentine's intonation remained authentic.

"Roger Specialist, I'm ready to do whatever I need to over there."

"I hope so…" He paused looking at my name-tape, as if he didn't know it before, "Harris… I hope so" He smiled and turned away, the big New Yorker followed. Without turning around, from down the hall, Valentine said in a loud voice, "See you in the D-Fac Cherry."

There was something about Valentine's demeanor that I hadn't yet seen in a soldier. I was too new to the army and to life to understand it at the time. I watched him walk down the hall. Almost a foot shorter than the soldier next to him, it was Valentine who somehow radiated with virility.

Van Dorn quickly interrupted my musings with his hot stinking breath, "Just me and you now Cherry." He looked eager, like a jail rapist after the guards left the shower. I looked right back into his thumbtack-sized eyeballs. I was a bit distracted by a greasy single strip of hair hovering above his caveman brow, but he responded abhorrently, "You eyeball fucking me Cherry?" The same question I was asked by my senior drill sergeant the first day of basic before he sent me to the concrete. There is no correct answer.

Timing is everything—a freshly showered Sergeant Eden came from his room. As he walked toward us Van

Dorn backed out of my face. I was relieved but knew I could count on a continuation of this charade at a later time. Approaching in an old gray Bruins T-shirt, black sweat pants and green socks, Sergeant Eden stood slightly over Van Dorn even in his Adidas soccer sandals. Sergeant Eden's olive drab eyes sat atop a thin Roman nose. His sparse eyebrows were barely visible with his blonde hair. He had a hard jaw line and his face was long and thin. His cheeks were high and masculine, but he wore an air of kindness around his mouth and eyes. He had a dip bottle like Dorn. But he took the cap off only to spit, and it didn't drip from the sides like Van Dorn's did. The tobacco was visible in his mouth only as a small bump on the left side of his bottom lip. His smile curved toward the side of his wad and he leaned his head slightly the opposite way, as if to counteract the weight. Just like James Dean did it with cigarettes, Sgt. Eden made chewing tobacco look cool. He exuded confidence. He nodded toward me as he walked up and looked at Van Dorn in his fresh uniform and said, "Dorn, fuck man, I forgot you had CQ tonight, that's fucked up. You got time to go eat with us before you got the desk?

"Always got the time for Alpha team. Just talking with the Cherry here." Sgt. Eden moved his tongue around his cheek, and said to me, "Hey, sorry I couldn't get here a little quicker for you." He chuckled with a mirthful look toward Van Dorn and said, "Let's go get some chow, I'm fucking starving man."

"Uh Sergeant, I was suppose to wait for Specialist

35

Tolson, he wanted to come with us. He's just taking a quick shower."

Van Dorn cut right in, "The way that motherfucker has at himself, it'll be another half hour. Fuck that, I got CQ duty in like half an hour, let's get the fuck outta here. He can catch up with y'all. I gotta get some fucking chow though."

Sgt. Eden was apprehensive. He spit into his bottle and said, "Yeah man, he's right. It's all good. He'll see us in the D-Fac, if we're still there." In the midst of stepping off, Eden wound up a wily kick and landed it right in Van Dorn's ass. As it landed he said, "Fucking Dorn. Fuckn' with the Cherry, always fuckn' with the Cherries." Van Dorn tried to block it nonchalantly, but to no avail.

He said back to Sgt. Eden, "I gotta get to 'em before you and Valentine soften 'em up."

"Where is Valentine anyway, he too good to eat with the team now?"

"Na, him and Ant were here, with me, they took off just a minute ago."

"Cause you're fucking with the Cherry. You know Valentine's not about that shit man." It's funny how in the army two people will just talk like you're not there. I just didn't matter enough yet.

The Dining Facility was exactly how one would imagine a cafeteria in a future dystopian military state. The obtrusively speckled linoleum tile, thin florescent light tubing possessing all the neon colors of the 1980s, architecturally decorative yet meaningless obtrusions jetting from the walls, pictures of the contemporary administration grinning with greed and false endowment. Army creeds, infantry creeds, airborne creeds, and ranger creeds, tactlessly camouflaging the otherwise demure wallpaper. The open setting exposed a kitchen full of cooks clad in woodland greens rather than chef whites. It had that strange amusement park feel of the battalion pt field.

It was only the second time I could remember having Salisbury steak, the other being in coach on my flight to Fort Benning. The meat was spongy and gray. A coagulated gravy-like sauce speckled with chunks of what I hoped were mushrooms further obscured the steak's taste, which was okay. Looking around the table, it seemed that I was the only person enjoying the savory dish. Van Dorn had a couple of grilled cheese sandwiches and a cup of cottage cheese and ketchup, Valentine, who we'd caught up with in line, had a salad, and Private First Class Antilli, I'll never forget Ant. PFC Antilli was the big dumb looking ambiguous solider who circled around me as part of Van Dorn's ruse just minutes before I was watching him with a double cheese burger in one hand and a half eaten hotdog in the other. Ant as he was called, had both elbows on the table, holding the burger and dog, one in each hand. He would curiously look at one item and then slowly pan to the other before ripping off a chunk. He didn't say a word or look away from his food the entire meal. That's how Ant was, one thing at a time. Antilli was big, dumb, and Italian, but hard as fuck.

Sgt. Eden and Van Dorn were going on about the

field exercise they had just completed. I was new, and felt only a part of something as far as my proximity was concerned. Sgt. Eden was cool, but it was obvious after just a few minutes, that while Van Dorn may have been a dick, he was definitely one of Sgt. Eden's boys. The two weeks training I had just missed was the topic of conversation for the better part of the meal, which only compounded my feelings of alienation. I was less apprehensive about all the training I missed than I was about the socialization. I saw my poorly timed arrival as missing the opportunity to become part of the team. But on top of that, there was the tactical issue. This was the battalion's last field problem before deployment. My first exercise with my squad would not be conducted under the comparatively safe confines of Fort Bragg. Afghanistan would be my first.

A paratrooper is measured by how much he can be trusted. If the paratrooper can be trusted to execute his mission with exact proficiency as dictated by his direct line supervisor, he may be referred to as a badass, a stud, a fucking killer, a steely-eyed-barrel-chested-flat-bellied-freedom-fighter of America. If the paratrooper cannot be trusted, he may be referred to as a shit bag, a shit bird, a piece of shit, a fuckup, a fuck stick, a blue falcon (buddy fucker), or simply a turd. I had heard dozens of these applications from Sgt. Eden and Van Dorn over dinner. Being a fuckup was a worse fate for a paratrooper than death.

As Van Dorn forcefully mixed as much ketchup as cottage cheese together in a cup, he went on about the field.

He was blunt. "This fucking PL man. I would just one fucking time like to see one of these West Point fuck ups come out squared away. I mean that shit with battalion headquarters, common, that's simple goddamn shit. I didn't know how to use the fucking radios when I first got here. But I was a private, not a fucking platoon leader. This motherfucker can't use a radio or read a fucking map. I was up there in the front on that movement. I heard him talking with SSG Reynolds. SSG Reynolds was being all business like, like he always fucking is, or I'd a torn into the Lieutenant's dumb ass. That guy needs to grow some fucking balls. And the Lieutenant, this fucking asshole didn't even have his compass declinated for Fort Bragg, he had that shit still set from Fort Benning. Fucker don't know you gotta change it. A fuckn'nother West Point shit bird." Sgt. Eden looked up at Van Dorn like he was the drunken cousin who went off about Dad at Christmas.

"Don't even worry about that shit Dorn, Lieutenant's going with third squad anyway. We just got SFC Holliday to deal with, I got him man." Van Dorn rolled his eyes and looked at me, "Yeah there's another asshole for you. Don't listen to this guy Cherry." Van Dorn pointed a spoon of cottage cheese at Sgt. Eden. "See SFC Holliday's got a hard on for our team leader here. Aint't that right Sergeant?" Sgt. Eden was unaffected by Van Dorn's fervor. He just coolly answered back, "The problem is that you southern rednecks just can't identify with a west coast man." He looked to me "You're from Oregon man, you'll be fine." My facial expression was caught between Dorn's sneer and Sgt. Eden's optimism. "See man, SFC Holliday is from SoCal. Now you don't necessarily have to be from SoCal too for him to like you. You don't even have to be from the West Coast really. Thing is man, if you come at him with that stinging southern twang like Dorn spits from between those redneck lips, then he's just not hearing you."

"Yeah, fucking bullshit if you ask me." Dorn rumbled away with a mouth full of food. "The bullshit with the Platoon Sergeant is that he assumes that just because he's a nigger I got a problem with him. You talk about us Dixie boys..." he leered at me, then Sgt. Eden, then back at me, "but you is the ones passing judgment about folks just 'cause they're from the South."

I couldn't tell if Sgt. Eden was put off. His expression said neutral, he just turned away and looked around the D-fac and said under his breath, "Jesus fucking Christ Van Dorn." Van Dorn just nodded as if somebody there were agreeing with what he said.

He went on. "Yeah, you see Cherry, Sgt. Eden here may as well be a fucking hippie. You boys can call it liberal or whatever the fuck. Seems to me ya'll just as well be a bunch of faggots."

Sgt. Eden's face was calm. He still had a little smile. "Ease up a bit Dorn, goddamn."

Dorn was the whole time wearing that same nasty grin, too small to be a smile but too sinister to be a smirk. "How about you Cherry, you one of them tree hugging faggots?"

40

"No Specialist, not me. I mean I care about the environment and all…" He cut me right off.

"Yeah all you fuckers from out west the same. If you ain't a faggot, you a hippie. How about it Cherry, which is it?"

I didn't know how much longer I could play it cool with him. I thought about smashing him across the face with my tray. Shit in the army is a lot like it is in prison from what I've heard. I thought maybe if I did fuck him up right then and there, I'd forever cement an irrevocable badass reputation for myself in battalion. Instead I just politely answered another bullshit question. "Well, I'm not gay Specialist. I guess I could have been considered kind of a hippie when I was in high school."

"When you was in high school? You mean like six months ago?" I had about two questions left in me. My impatience came out in my next response. "A lot has happened in those six months Specialist." He dropped his spoon to his tray and leaned forward into my face. I was admittedly nervous. I thought again about the tray option. He sprayed a bit of tobacco at my face as he talked, but I didn't flinch. "Oh yeah, you got you a ride to Afghanistan now Cherry, WHHHEEE YEAH! I hope you ready Cherry. No, I'm just teasing you, you be fine." I wanted to punch him in the teeth as he reached his hand over the table, but instead I met his fist with mine in a gesture of good faith. "Welcome to first platoon Cherry. Sergeant, I see you later." With a nod to Sgt. Eden and a wink to me, Dorn left the table just as my new roommate, Tolson, came over. He had that happy, relaxed, and shy look about him that said he'd just jerked off. He plopped down on the bench. He dropped his tray on the table, and started up right away, "Hey what's going on? I'm fucking spent. That extra eight hundred rounds of ammo slows a motherfucker's pace."

"Extra eight hundred rounds?" I asked.

"Yeah, see I am the automatic rifleman for bravo team. That means that I deliver accurate suppressive or direct fire at a rate of one thousand rounds per minute from up to and including one thousand meters. That means I got to carry a lot of ammo, eight hundred fucking rounds. In Afghanistan, we're going to carry twice that, sixteen hundred fucking rounds. That's a lot of fucking ammo, and that's why an automatic rifleman is the baddest motherfucker on the battle field." Tolson had just given me my all time favorite description of the squad automatic weapon. I coveted the weapon and the position it carried immediately.

Finished with his food, Sgt. Eden wiped the corners of his mouth and threw his napkin down on to his tray with vigor. He pulled out his can of Copenhagen longcut, slapped his index finger hard against the side three times, and stuffed a wad into his lip all in one motion. Holding his tray in one hand and standing up he reached his fist out to Tolson's as Tolson's came up to meet his. "You sound a bit worked up from the field still man. You should have taken another go around man. Gotta remember Tolson, when in doubt, jerk it out." We all laughed, Sgt. Eden smiled and said, "Take it easy fellas. Harris, get with me tomorrow. In his best Patton impersonation, he uttered, "Won't be long now boys." I watched Sgt. Eden walk out of the dining hall, cool, confident, and humble all at once.

Tolson sat down across from me. "Well you enjoy your dinner with Dorn? Kind of prick ain't he? But Eden's a good shit yeah?" A good shit? I thought to myself. "Yeah he is. Specialist Van Dorn though, I don't know."

"I wouldn't worry about him too much, as long as you got Eden on your side, your gravy. Just between you and me Cherry, first squad is Eden's squad. Reynolds doesn't run shit. Lyons is in charge of bravo team, but I'm telling you, it's the Eden show when it really comes down to it. You'll see man, it's always him in the squad leader meeting. When we go to the field, well you won't see that I guess, but when we're in Afghanistan, watch, it will be Eden mapping out the patrol routes and giving the fucking operation orders. Fuck Dorn, don't worry about him."

"Why is it like that, if Sgt. Eden is actually in charge, why don't they just make him the squad leader?"

"Fuck, it just doesn't work like that. I mean if you get your sergeant stripes, they'll give you a fire team but that jump up to squad leader is a lot fucking different. You need to have more time in, second enlistment usually. Mostly though, we have too many fucking staff sergeants in the Company and nowhere to put them. There's just no way a buck sergeant is going to run a fucking squad. Besides, with Lyons in the fucking platoon," Tolson paused for a second to pour some Louisiana hot sauce on what looked like a burrito but could have been a rubber chew toy. It struck me out of nowhere and I interrupted Tolson right away, "Oh yeah yeah yeah yeah, that reminds me, somebody came to our room right after you left for the shower." Already knowing, Tolson asked in a somber voice, "Fucking who?"

"Well I don't really know but I think it must have been Sgt. Lyons."

"Son of a bitch. What the fuck does he want now?"

"He was pretty pissed off. He made me do pushups..."

"What the fuck did he want, what did he say?" Tolson was getting firey quickly.

"He asked where you were and I told him that you were in the shower. I told him that I was going to go to the D-Fac with you and he told me to tell you to go back to your room and wait for him immediately, that he'd be by for you."

"What the fuck?! FUCK, FUCK FUUUCK! It's not you Cherry. It's just that, you don't know Lyons yet, but you will man, he's just such a miserable fucking asshole, and he has to make shit fucked up for everybody. Thing is, I don't have the slightest fucking clue what he could be pissed about either. I fucking hate him. Everybody does."

"He's like that with everybody? Anybody hang out with him outside of work?" Tolson shook his head. "Fuck man, he hangs out with this dude in bravo who I guess he went to airborne school with, but fuck no. Everybody hates his ass. He's got a banging wife though. But she's one of those hot little bitches, all polished up all the time. You can tell just by looking at her that she's a little cunt. I don't know what his fucking problem is. Fuck him. I'm taking this burrito to go. I've got to get back to the room." Gesturing with his head for me to quickly follow, Tolson said with a mouthful of food, "He'll skin both our asses if he goes there and we're not back."

By the time we got out the door of the D-Fac, it was if nothing had or would happen. Tolson was the kind of guy who was able to reserve an inexplicable passion for his job as a soldier while at the same time exercising his own will with an almost complete absence of formality. He was a Nietzschean soldier if one could be imagined, between Dionysus and Apollo, torn between passionate intoxication and aimed reason, born of tragedy. His beret was not fitted in the same way as Dorn's and the rest of Alpha team's. His looked more like mine, crooked with blots of fuzz hanging off. His uniform was not pressed. His boots got shined bi-weekly, he shaved every other day, his hair was always just too long, and whenever he could he had a cigarette in his lips. I always liked being with Tolson, despite his boisterousness, he was somehow calming to walk and talk with. When he stepped his head bobbed up and down while his neck waved in a slight S motion, it was if he always had music playing in his head and was just casually keeping the beat. With his long arms and legs, and him being as thin as he was, he gave the appearance of being much taller than he was in actuality. At first glance you'd no doubt peg him for a least 6' 2" but when I got up on him, he was at least

45

three inches shorter, my height at best. His hair was cut once a week, one of the standards he usually met, but it was always out of regulation. If we had to have it just above the ear, Tolson's was just past.

"So what's up man, you got a girl back home or what, where are you from by the way?"

"I'm from Oregon. No, I don't have a girlfriend. Well, I mean I do, but you know, I'm here. She's in Oregon."

"Yeah which means somebody else'll be fucking her here soon. You got a picture of her man?" I had a picture of her from our junior year in her cheerleading uniform that I carried in my wallet. I think that's why I was with her in the first place. I wasn't a football star, but I still fucked the cheerleading captain.

"Yeah, this was a couple years ago."

Tolson grabbed the photo form my hand. "Holy shit man, this your girl? I may be going AWOL man, tell her you died in the war, go comfort her and shit. What the fuck are you doing here?" Everyone who saw her picture said something like that. I had only one answer.

"To go to combat." Tolson responded more colorfully, albeit, the same as most had.

"When you got pussy like that at home, what the fuck you trying to fuck with all this shit for? I'd be up in that shit all day every fucking day."

I couldn't believe the balls on some of these guys, calling me a faggot, saying they were going to fuck my girlfriend. I guess with Tolson it was okay, when he said it I could chuckle it off, with Dorn, I wanted to gouge out his eyes. "Yeah, well I don't know. She says that she loves me and will wait. And I believe her, she wouldn't... she's just not the cheating type." Tolson didn't want to tell me that I was fucked. "We're gonna be gone for at least six months you know?"

"I know. I've already been gone for six."

Walking up to the top floor where first platoon stayed, we passed already drunk paratroopers in groups of three and four on all the stair landings. Everybody had bottles of beer. Some had a cigarette in their free hand. Some had a bottle of whiskey. I heard a shout from just below us, "YEAH, first platoon's got a new cherry. Bring him back down here Tolson, let us have a taste."

Tolson's big screen projection TV was still on when we walked back in the room. As he opened the door, there before me on the giant muted screen was a man standing on a coffee table fucking a girl in a panda suit from behind while she was peeling a banana. He didn't act embarrassed, he didn't rush to go turn it off, he didn't do shit, he just casually pointed to the other side of the room and said, "Yeah you probably figured it out by now, but that's your wall locker, you got top bunk. You want to watch a movie or something?"

"Yeah, that sounds cool, what all you got?" The whole time the man was still plowing away on screen, he didn't give a shit, he just answered back, "All kinds of shit man. What kind of movie you going for?" For some reason, the whole thing made me strangely comfortable, more than I'd been in a long time. I relaxed back into one of the two lawn chairs that sat side by side in front of his TV.

"Personally man, I could use a comedy. Just got here yesterday and it's been pretty crazy so far."

"You like Bill Murray?"

"Pete Venkman, hell yeah man."

Tolson was puzzled. He inquired with a scrunched brow, "Pete Venkman?" He paused and upon realization he pumped his fists next to his side with his thumbs up. "Oh, yeah, yeah, yeah, nice, fucking Ghostbusters, duh. You down to watch Stripes then?"

"Seems appropriate." He excitingly pulled the DVD from its slot, stopped for a moment, and asked, "Say man, you want a drink? I got some fucking Jim Beam and a few kinds of beer. Oh and yeah, you probably don't have any fucking food or anything yet?"

"No I haven't even gone to a store or anything."

"Good, don't. There's all kinds of shit in the fridge that you can help me get rid of before we leave. Want a beer, or some Beam maybe?"

"No, thanks man, this weekend for sure."

Tolson smiled at me as if he knew I would succumb, "May not be a weekend man."

He pulled the frost covered half-gallon from the freezer, and filled his glass about half full. He opened up a can of Coke, poured it to nearly the top, and then chugged what was left in the can. He finished his cocktail with a couple ounce pour of Nyquil, stirring the whole thing with his finger then shaking it dry. I had never seen something like that in my life, my face told the same story I guess. Tolson took it halfway down in the first drink and said, "It actually tastes really fucking good, and it'll put you to sleep too, trust me." My clouded response was cut off by the same fierce knock I heard an hour before.

I sat closer to the door and I looked back at Tolson. Giving me a mixed and hesitated gesture that meant to open the door, I took a shallow breath and opened it right as Sgt. Lyons was about to land his fist again. His eyes were far apart and his short broad nose rested between his deep chasms of eye sockets. His brow was prominent and thick with light brown hair and his cheeks were high. His jaw was wide, square, and matched his half-back frame all the way down. He might have been better looking if he wasn't squeezing that pit bull look onto his face. But it was definitely what he was going for.

"CHERRY! The second motherfucker I wanted to see." He looked past my shoulder to see Tolson in the room as well. "And YOU—SPECIALIST, you can just start pushing right now." The smallest sigh from Tolson barely whispered past my ear, but it caught Sgt. Lyons' loud and clear. He grabbed my collar by both hands, and threw me to the side against the wall locker. Dashing toward Tolson who was face down doing pushups, he drove his knee into Tolson's side, but Tolson kept his balance and continued to push. Then, on his knees, Sgt. Lyons brought his face to the level of Tolson's, moving up and down with him as the exercise dictated. "You want to huff and puff at me Specialist? You want to show this new private, YOUR FUCKING ROOMATE, that the chain of command don't mean shit in first platoon? You better get the fuck disciplined Tolson. I'm tired of fucking telling your ass." He whipped his body around like he was going to introduce me into the ring.

He came at me like a bull. "And you, what the fuck Cherry? You're going to let your boy push while you stand there with your thumb up your fucking pussy? GET THE FUCK DOWN AND PUSH CHERRY? Now ya'll better wake the fuck up. I'm telling you right now. Tolson, you better wire your shit tight, right fucking now. And you, Cherry, don't be thinking that you're gonna be hiding behind Eden's fucking ass, I got you motherfucker." Tolson and I were facing each other and continued to do push-ups as Sgt. Lyons stood stationary between the two of us, yelling at one of us for a few seconds and suddenly whipping around to the other. Occasionally, and only when he was really driving home his sentence, he would yell straight ahead as if face to face with an invisible adversary. "Now for the reason I fucking came here initially. Specialist Tolson, would you mind telling me what bravo team's standard operating procedure is for weapons maintenance and weapons turn in upon returning from a live fire exercise or field problem?"

"I know, I just gave them to Browning because—"

"SHUT THE FUCK UP SPECIALIST. The question I asked was regarding our SOP for weapons turn in, not your fucking bullshit reason why you defied my orders, Specialist. Now what is bravo team's SOP for weapons turn in upon returning from a live fire exercise or field problem?"

"Everyone cleans and turns in his own weapon, Sergeant."

"Why the fuck then did I come down from the squad leader's office and find Browning standing in the arm's room line with Ant's 203 and your SAW?"

"I gave Browning our weapons so Ant could go down to the motor pool to link up with maintenance to get some more screws for our helmet's, and I needed to link up with commo for new batteries for the radios."

"Don't get fucking smart with me Specialist. There's a fucking chain of command and I'm at the end of it, roger?" Your new fucking boyfriend here is gonna get his head blown off the first day we're in country because his piece of shit roommate taught him to say, 'fuck orders' and 'fuck the chain of command.'" He abruptly stormed out throwing the door shut behind him. We were still pushing as it slammed closed.

"That motherfucker. Like I said man, you'll get to know Lyons." Tolson was flustered. For Tolson, that kind of shit was harder than any forced march, ten mile run, or obstacle course—swallowing it up. He ripped his shirt off and threw it atop his wall locker. Reaching for his Nyquil cocktail, he plopped down in his chair and took a sip. "You sure you don't want a fucking drink?"

"Yeah I guess I'll take a beer. Fuck it, give me a shot of Beam too."

Division was building us new barracks for when we got back. That was the first and only night I slept in that room. The next afternoon we left for Afghanistan.

PART II

COMBAT

FIREBASE GARDEZ

Firebase Gardez was home to fifty-five personnel. This included our ten-man element from Alpha Co., a thirty man platoon from Charlie Co. and two armored crews from Delta Co. equaling another eight men. There were also two medics and three Afghani civilians who acted as our interpreters, and two men working under the orders of an undisclosed government organization.

At the time the army had about a dozen of what they referred to as firebases, and later forward observation bases, or FOBs. These firebases were a micro version of major airbases such as the ones in Kabul and Kandahar. Where Kabul and Kandahar had multiple facilities, capabilities to land fixed wing aircrafts, and housed 20,000 or more troops, firebases like the one in Gardez, had no facilities, no running water, a couple of generators at best, and held less than one hundred men. Of these hundred or so men, the vast majority were elite infantrymen, special operation soldiers, or support attachments with equivalent combat training. Firebases were far reaching outposts that served as the staging ground for offensive operations. Life in Kandahar Airbase was relatively safe -- twice as safe as many of our urban communities. Out at the firebases, like the one in Gardez, life was fragile.

Firebase Gardez was located about a mile outside the city of Gardez, which had a population of about 60,000. The city sits almost two miles above sea level at the edge of the Hindu Kush Mountain Range, an offshoot of the Himalayas and the second largest mountain range in the world. Between the city and the Hindu Kush, was Firebase Gardez. Just off the Pakistan border, Firebases Gardez, Shkin, and Orgun-E were considered most likely to destroy insurgencies that were central to the operations of both the Taliban and Al Qaeda. Along the border in 2003, Osama Bin Laden and friends were priority number one. A year before our arrival, he escaped the attacks at Tora Bora and was thought to be operating in the area, using the Pakistani border as his safety net. These firebases were placed strategically near the border of Pakistan, between Kabul in the north and Kandahar in the south, in hopes of intercepting Bin Laden, or at the very least, stifling the Taliban's capabilities. We spent two days in Kandahar, a few meals, and some bullets, then out to Gardez. Later that year Time magazine would headline the Paktia Province of Afghanistan as, "The Most Dangerous Place on Earth," it was to be our home for the next four months.

Nothing came in as I sucked air upon exiting the Chinook. My heart pounded as we hit the ground, we piled out, and in less than a minute the bird was back off the ground. Our team was first out the door. I followed Sgt. Eden and Valentine. Van Dorn was to my rear. I thought my knees were going to buckle from the weight. All my shit weighed somewhere between one hundred-twenty and one hundred-forty pounds. All on my back. We landed only about a quarter mile from the firebase and were within the cover of the two turrets that we could see from the ground.

Briefed and fitted in Kandahar for just two days before being dropped off in Gardez, the air did nothing for our lungs yet. When you're that high up, you can breathe just as easily. It's not that it's harder to take in the air. It's that the air you do breathe in does nothing for you. Imagine being completely out of breath, gasping desperately and painfully for oxygen as you huffed down empty breaths. It feels like you're being suffocated really slowly with a plastic bag. I ran straight out from the Chinook as we dropped off. After just fifty yards, I had to drop to the prone position to catch my breath. There was nobody in front of me, and nobody on my sides. The scene was like nothing I had seen before. There were mountains all around, snow capped by the December storms. The geography combines the high deserts of Nevada with the Rocky Mountains of Colorado, except the mountains were bigger and rockier, and the desert much higher. Looking around I thought it must have been a training ground engineered by the military as a simulation of the harshest environment imaginable. I caught my breath and rolled over to my side to look behind me and saw three groups resting on their knees. Sgt. Eden's words were drowned out by the whirling chops of the Chinook propeller but I could see his arm motioning for me to get to him. I used all my force to control my huge pack and push myself back up on my feet. I felt like a desert tortoise. When I got back with the team, I still couldn't hear anything Sgt. Eden was saying but I could see SFC Holliday using hand signals to let us know to move forward in a wedge formation, that our attachments were to follow, and that bravo team was to pick up the rear. We walked at a speed no quicker than you would walk if you were on your way to the bank, but it was taking every ounce of our energy to keep the pace. I remember looking out the door as we were landing and taking a breath of relief at how close we were. With those combat loads and that air, the quarter mile turned into many.

Firebase Gardez was at one time clearly inhabited by a very small element of locals, probably a large family or a group of farmers. Before US military arrival, there was just one structure to the compound. A very large two level house made from dried clay and brick, well structured and architecturally sound, but rough on the outside. The house made a giant L shape. The long side was about one hundred and fifty feet. The short side about half that. There were multiple rooms and each had blue painted wooden doors that led back outside. The windows weren't of glass, but instead had swinging blue wooden shades that opened and closed.

The second story was built atop the short side, and had a fifty-foot tower on its edge. The long side was just one story, but you could utilize the roof as another platform. The longer side also had a tower that matched the height of the other at about fifty feet from the ground. The towers had sturdy wooden ladders built along the sides. We had reinforced them with sandbags and placed a 240-B machine gun in each one as guard turrets for the firebase. From the southern tower you had a full view of the city. At a mile away it always looked peaceful. Green tracers would light up the night sky daily. The hot smell of bread and spice was faintly caught in the breeze. The shots fired sounded distant and popped in the air. The tower provided distance and the illusion of safety making it tolerable to isolate yourself in a little box in the sky.

From the north tower you faced the mountain ridge. Out of the three hundred-sixty degrees that surrounded us, about seventy percent of it was mountain edge. The rest was the edge of the city. It was flat where we were, already two miles up, and the mountains around us went up a mile or two higher so you felt especially tiny within the backdrop. The valley floor was speckled with small bushes and shrubs or bluish-greens that broke up the plain dusty brown of the scene. There were no streams, no creeks, no brooks or channels, but it was beautiful in its way. The way the setting sun fell upon the ascending mountaintops at dawn told you that while you were closer to hell than ever, the view of heaven had never been so clear. Brilliant shades of sunlight snuck through the crevasses between the mountain peaks. Even after the sun fell below the horizon, the reds, purples, and oranges it left behind would for the greatest minute coalesce in a blazing afterglow. It would have, if not for the context, been a beautiful scene. But in a way it still was, maybe even more so.

The big two-story house was the center of Firebase Gardez. Along the perimeter, about seventy-five yards from the structure was a wall built out of hescos. Hescos are giant sandbags that stand about six and a half feet high. A thin but strong wire forms a grid pattern in the shape of giant cubes. The hescos are lined with a near indestructible gray fabric. They're open on each end, one open end on the ground, and one facing up. The hescos can then be filled with dirt, essentially making them giant sandbags.

As we were one of the first units to use Firebase Gardez, we built the place. This consisted of digging shit holes, constructing piss tubes, digging mortar pits and ammo storages, constructing an additional guard tower, digging two attack bunkers, and constructing additional sandbag walls around the old WWII tents we slept in. We shat in one of three holes with ply-wood built around them. We pissed in a configuration of tubes. To piss a soldier put his dick in the open end of a four inch wide PVC pipe that comes at him at a about a thirty degree angle. There were seven of these pipes originating from a center and protruding out in a circle at an equal distance apart from one another. We only had meals ready to eat (MREs), we had bottled water when we were lucky, and when we weren't, we had to boil water over a fire from the nearby well. We cleaned our clothes maybe monthly, and by hand. We didn't shower. There was one phone, no internet, and the mail came with resupply from Kandahar once every three weeks.

We had three interpreters. In 2003 the military industrial complex had not yet reached the height to provide the privatized military resources that it would later on allocate for the war. We had to be old school about it. We got our own interpreters. These men were not American citizens who had formal training in the local languages of

Pashtun and Dari. Our interpreters came from Gardez. All three were born and raised in the city in which they would later aid American forces in combating the previously dominate Taliban. For this they all had prices on their heads. Assisting the American forces in any way meant exposing yourself to the Taliban. Many in the cities viewed the interpreters as traitors to both their country and religion. Supporting the infidels against fellow Muslims meant bringing great danger to both yourself and your family. These were the real people with something at stake.

First squad had Farid. Farid was young, just at drinking age if he were in America, and with all the intellect and ambition to thrive if he had been given what I was at birth. But Farid's time and place provided more trying matters for his concern. Farid didn't love America. He loved the people of Afghanistan, but he found with us something that the Taliban could not offer him, economic stability.

I remember SFC Holliday bringing him into our tent just a couple of days after we arrived in Gardez. We were in our tent, which was exactly like five others spread around the firebase. The tents were not placed in any particular pattern like you might imagine. Instead, each tent was spaced enough apart so that a single rocket would only take out one at a time. With the uneven ground of the valley floor, the tents looked scattered almost randomly throughout the firebase. Our squad's tent was between the hescos and the northern guard tower, just far enough from the hescos not to take debris from a blast on the wall, and far enough away from the guard tower to not be effected by its potential destruction and collapse. When constructing Firebase Gardez, everything was considered in hopes that no more than ten people would be killed at one time.

Farid walked in ahead of SFC Holliday. He didn't look apprehensive as you might imagine, his face was young but spirited. He was tall with the slender but strong build of a wide receiver. He didn't wear the traditional garb of the Afghan male. He had the same dessert issue boots that we all wore. His laces were tucked in with no careless ends. His pants were woodland green cargos, the same as we wore when we trained back at Bragg. He had on a black fleece pullover not unlike one you would see in a Seers catalogue. His eyes were covered by black Oakley wraparounds, and a black fleece beanie crowned his head. His beard was long but sparse and could be barely noticed with the ragged white scarf wrapped around his neck. He wore a curious smile, and didn't take off his glasses, so as he continually panned around the tent, his eyes never became fixed upon any one individual.

Standing just behind with his hand on his shoulder, SFC Holliday introduced him to the almost bewildered squad. "This is our interpreter, Farid. He's going to be going with us on any missions or patrols that we'll be doing while we're here. SSG Reynolds, team leaders, come up here and I'll brief you on the details." I was overcome. They never told us that we'd be working with a local. I was about to clean my rifle when they came in, I remember clenching my pistol grip when I saw him.

Sitting on my bunk, I faced Browning as we bullshitted about nonsense and cleaned our weapons. Browning was the second newest guy in the squad and made a quick ally in Gardez. He had slid the M203 grenade launcher from off the barrel of his rifle and pressed the hollow tube against his army issued lens as if it were a telescope fixed upon our new interpreter. As he mockingly gazed I asked, "See anything there, Brownie?"

"Looks alright from here, but Afghani or not, bitch better keep a tight grip on them Oakleys." Everything Browning said was taken in jest. That's usually the way he meant it. He had only come to the unit a couple of months before me, but was already loved. He was my counterpart in bravo team. Browning's mix of goofiness and witty charm brought laughs to a place where they were otherwise scarce. He always carried about his business completely unaffected by the goings on around him. Being in Afghanistan never took away from his campy demeanor. I asked him, "What do you think SFC Holliday tells them that they don't tell us?" Browning mockingly widened his eyes and twisted his body around toward the leader's congregation.

"Probably how long we're actually gonna be out on these missions. Figure out how long we're gonna be out there, then figure out how long to tell us we're gonna be out there."

"Yeah no shit, it took me a minute to figure that one out. Let's see, the first one we did was supposed to be a continued twenty hours, we ended up being out for four days. Then when we went to the pass -- that was supposed to be two days. It ended up being seven and then the last one was only supposed to be a day, and it was almost three fucking days later we finally got back and got to sleep." Browning had finished reassembling his weapon and was performing a functions check so as to make sure it was proper. Sliding his action back and forth and the sound of his grenade launcher opening and closing, the slapping of metal parts, created a sound more sweat to the infantryman's ear than a Brazilian rainforest.

Some people sleep to whale songs or waterfalls. I could have fallen asleep to those metallic notes any night. I said, "That's a lot of oil you put on your bolt man. Doesn't it collect too much dirt and shit when it's like that?" He took off his glasses and leaned forward as if what he were about to say were really important. He held his glasses and used them to point as he explicated his point, "Fuck all that, you gotta keep that shit wet Harris. Some of these guys will tell you differently, but don't listen to that bullshit. They'll tell you bullshit about how you need to keep that shit clean, 'a drop will do you' and all that bullshit, well fuck all that, I want my shit wet, roger. It might stay a bit cleaner, but the shit won't work, who gives a fuck how clean it is, if you can't get that bitch open when you need her to. I keep my bitch wet at all times, she may pick up a few more stragglers than some of the other guys, but you just need to make sure you maintain that shit, take care of that bitch. But trust me Harris, don't let that bitch dry up on you, always keep her wet."

"That goes for your sister too?" Browning had a hot sister, a year younger than us, seventeen, he made the mistake of showing a family photograph the first week we were in country. He heard something about her every day since. Still facing each other, Browning had his back turned to the leaders' meeting that looked to be wrapping up. He jokingly jumped off his bunk and came to a wrestling position. Browning was about my size, 5' 11' about 175, his hair was blonde though, and curly unlike mine. He flipped his cot over with exaggerated fury, like a WWF wrestler pumping up the crowd before stepping into the ring. I jumped off my bed and replicated his stance. We caused a bit of a stir, and everybody in the tent was watching us. Sgt. Lyons was, as usual, the guy to put a stop to our jesting. SFC Holliday, SSG Reynolds, and Sgt. Eden were laughing.

"GET THE FUCK DOWN, THE BOTH OF YOU. You two shitfucks wanna jerk each other off, I got something for you." The meeting had ended, and had it not been for Sgt. Eden, Sgt. Lyons might have had Browning and me pushing for the next hour. Sgt. Eden was as serious about being a paratrooper as any soldier, but he let things like that go. He understood the role of morale in a place like that. He rolled his eyes at Sgt. Lyons like he was the kid asking about homework. "It's fine, not now, let's just get this info out." Sgt. Eden didn't like guys disciplining his soldiers, and Sgt. Lyons didn't like guys questioning his methods.

"Eden, you wanna fucking tit feed your soldiers, that's your business. But don't step on my fucking toes when I'm trying to instill discipline." Without raising his voice at all, Sgt. Eden sternly said, "Browning's your guy, roger? You go do whatever the fuck you want with him over there. Harris is my guy though, and I have information for my soldiers." Sgt. Lyons shook his head at Sgt. Eden and gave both Browning and I the command to recover, which despite Sgt. Eden's words, I waited for. As Sgt. Eden started to brief us, I looked over at Sgt. Lyons who was already beaming across at me as he slowly tapped his chest and mouthed the words "I got your ass."

ALL THE LIVE LONG DAY

For our first two weeks in Gardez, our primary mission, behind holding down the firebase, was to actually construct the firebase. We had done a few patrols and some small mission, but they hadn't yet yielded the dangerous excitement I had been promised. We had to return fire a few times, but the first hostile shots from my rifle were superficial counters to small groups of men, maybe two to four at a time, firing from a far. It was crazy seeing them though, the enemy. They weren't cut out silhouette targets on a range at Fort Benning, or Crazy Ivans at Bragg. The Crazy Ivan thing actually calls for a bit of explanation.

During the end of the Cold War era the Army used targets that were cut outs of cartooned short fat men with small mustaches and huge grins. A kind of Anti-Communist propaganda picture of what a Russian would look like I guess, 'Crazy Ivans'. I never got a fixed shot in those first couple of weeks, but I knew I wasn't shooting at Crazy Ivans anymore. These targets moved and they breathed too, sometimes you could see it in the cold air. They were mostly tall and slender in appearance, however their tall appearance was usually just illusory, their skinny bodies and turbans made them look a lot taller than they actually were. Most of them were older than me and had short hair and long pointed beards. They wore what we called man dresses, always colored with earthy tones; they were called Shalwar Kameezs by locals, a kind of suit, pants and top. The bottoms, which were a pajama like pant, very baggy and spacious at the top, narrowing as they approached the bottom until the cuffs of the pants fitted to the ankles. The top is just a really big and long full-length sleeve shirt; they were always split about halfway up the side, making them even looser fitting. Some wore boots they had taken from dead soldier, but most, even in winter, wore traditional open-toed strap sandals. If you saw guys on a downtown patrol wearing boots it perked up your attention. On their heads was usually either a turban or a small hat called a pakul. Their eyes were black, and so usually was their hair, except with some, whom appeared to be the likely offspring of an Afghani mother and a Russian rapist soldier father. And they all moved very quickly. We would work on our bunkers and the hescos, and they would choose opportune times to take a few shots at somebody standing out in the open for too long. It became like a game. Dig, dig, dig, some shots fired, drop the rifle, fire a couple of rounds back in the general direction. Then dig,

dig, dig, all over again, rinse and repeat. We took no casualties, and as far as I know we inflicted none either. For that first two weeks I was a paratrooper after I was a construction worker. I knew that this building and digging time could be made to my advantage though. I had just gotten to the unit and I hadn't performed any real infantry tactics for months, but I could dig with the best of them. I used this time to establish myself as a willing and strong worker. I also used it to establish a few relationships, for better, or for worse.

Every squad had its individual tasks in which it was responsible for. The goal was that after two weeks, we would have two mortar pits dug, three shitters, piss tubes, hescos all around the perimeter, guard towers, two ammo bunkers, an MRE and water bunker, and enough personnel bunkers to hold everybody in the firebase. The mortar men had it the worst. They were responsible for both of their pits, easily the biggest area to dig out of any of the endeavors. SFC Holliday volunteered our squad to dig out their second pit so they could focus on an ammo bunker for their rounds. The pits were to be as roundly shaped as possible, which given SFC Holliday's expectations, a perfect circle, twenty-five feet wide, and three feet deep, so it was a lot of fucking dirt. It wasn't complicated, just keep the outside of the whole nice and round, and just dig for an extended amount of time. We worked in pairs. One person dug with an entrenching tool while the other held the sandbag. When the sandbag was full it was stacked off to the side and used as fortification on one of the many areas of the firebase that called for fortification. I held while Valentine dug, Dorn held while Sgt. Eden dug, Sgt. Lyons held for Ant, Browning held for Tolson. And SFC Holliday and SSG Reynolds stacked the filled bags. It was cold, maybe forty degrees in the day. The work kept us warm enough to not need field jackets, but we still wore our issued silk long underwear and black fleece beanies. We had been away from the luxuries afforded to us in the States for only a week at this time, so it was pussy I think we were talking about.

Antilli talked like he got a lot of it, and maybe he did, everybody listened to his stories like they were true. It didn't matter. He was very boisterous when he spoke, especially when he was talking about fucking.

There were ten of us digging, filling sandbags, talking shit, and exchanging lies about sexual conquests. At this point, we were still unaffected by Gardez . I remember that moment as one of the last that allowed me to forget about my unsavory disposition. As was often the case during these discourses, the floor belonged to Antilli. He was a twenty-one year old burly New York Italian. He acted like The Fonz and looked like him too, only with black hair, trimmed to a high and tight. His moniker was a shortened version of his surname, but it carried more meaning. Ants can carry as much as fifty times their body weight, according to some of the guys, so could Antilli. He spoke with a low roar and a thick Bensonhurst accent. He pumped out his chest when he had a crowd, always with a Marlboro Red bouncing from his lips as he rumbled away with his sonorous tales.

"So I was a senior, and this bitch was a junior. I was giving it to her best friend a month or so before I started fuckn' her. They was both cheerleadas. Blonde hair, big titted hard-bodies, the both of 'em. Her friend figured out I was fuckn' her to get to her friend—so she was fuckn' gone, fuckn' outta there. Thought I was out both pieces of pussy till her friend sees me at this party and is blowing me in my buddy's car an hour later. And this bitch could suck a fuckn' dick. Let me tell you, thought she was going to suck both my nuts right out the end of my cock."

"Keep fucking digging Ant, or shut the fuck up!" Sgt. Lyons was the only one not overtaken with Ant's story enough to let him lean against his E-tool while the rest of us worked.

"You got it Sergeant." Ant speared the spade deep into the ground a couple of times, and went back to his story.

"So anyhow, like I was saying, this bitch is on my dick like a bum on a bologna sandwich. Now remember, I borrowed my buddy's car so I could go get a hummer from this bitch." I paused for a moment to pull out his pack of cigarettes and light another up. I did the same. "So this bitch stops and starts jerking me off and tells me to let her know when I'm gonna blow my load and shit, right. So I'm in the driver seat, with my back all pressed up against the door, and this bitch is in the passenger seat all leaned over on my dick and shit, right. So I'm getting ready, you know the shits working up, she's all the way down on my cock,

70

I'm talking lips down on the root, and right as I'm about to tell her I'm gonna come, I feel myself fall backward as somebody's ripping the door open. I'm right there, you know, just about to bust, so when the door comes open, as I fall back, BAM, I shoot right in her fuckn' mouth. Now I'm on my back looking up at my ex-girlfriend and the brother of the bitch who's got a mouth full of my come. They was at the same party, saw us leave, and fuckn' followed us. So I'm on my fuckn' back, legs in the car, still got my pants down and my dick out. Right when this bitch's brother Tommy bends down to grab me up, his sister leans over and spewes my come all over this asshole's face. My ex-girlfriend is all yelling and shit, still standing next to him, saying she's gonna fucking kill me and shit, well, he's still got my come all over his fuckn' face so he turns and fuck'n pukes right down my ex-girlfriend's tits. I roll off to the side, and this bitch has the other bitch by the hair and is pulling her outta the fuck'n car now. Dude's on his hands and knees, shirt off, wiping his face, puking all over the goddamn place, the two bitches are out the car pulling on each other's hair, so I jump back in and take off back to the party. Fucked some other broad later that night."

Ant plunged his E-tool into the dug up soil and tossed a shovel full at Browning who was mockingly making a jerk-off motion at him with his hand. Browning playfully ducked the dirt, and returned a load right back at Ant. "KNOCK IT THE FUCK OFF. If you can't bullshit and work at the same time, then we'll work in silence." Sgt.

Lyons' expression didn't change at any point during Ant's story. I know because I watched.

"Common guys, we got a lot of shit to dig here." SFC Holliday was satisfied with our pace just fine. He was keeping Sgt. Lyons at bay. Valentine got the conversation started back. He asked, "So Ant, how many girls you say you had sex with then?" Everybody looked up at him. "Shit Val, what kind of a question is that? That's like asking how many people are in Yankee stadium, or how many times we won the pennant."

Browning chimed in, "Actually it's nothing like that Ant, those are actual figures that can be easily calculated, whereas none of us have a scale here to weigh out exactly how much bullshit's in each one of your claims."

"You don't gotta believe me Brownie, just take your sister's word for it."

"Watch it Ant, that's taking it too far, you know my family doesn't fuck dumb grease ball Italians."

"Ohhhhh." That was it. Ant had nothing else. Browning smiled with satisfaction, and his concentration went back to digging. His smile lingered for minutes afterward. Antilli wasn't done bantering though, he turned to me.

"What's up with you there Cherry, I heard you got some hot pussy waiting for you back home. Where is it you from Cherry, Arkansas or some shit." I was surprised to have the conversation go to me but responded back.

"Oregon actually." They could have probably bordered each other as far as Ant knew.

"Oregon, what the fuck you got in Oregon?"

"Oh, I don't know man, lot of stuff. I mean you like outdoor kind of stuff?" Ant just leaned back and laughed as loud as a fire engine. "Outdoor, shit Cherry. Outdoor, shit, that means stickball where I'm from." Everybody but Sgt. Lyons, Browning and I, laughed.

"Yeah like baseball, but like in the street, right? I've seen people play on TV and stuff, but I've never played. It looks way cool."

"You ain't need to play stickball when you got grass Cherry. All kinds of shit like that in Oregon, huh?"

"Well yeah man, you know, it's not like the East Coast I guess. More land and stuff. I went to New York though, when I was like fourteen, it's really cool." Dorn handed a filled bag to SFC Holliday and chimed in. "So, you play baseball then Cherry?"

"Yeah, since I was a kid, all through high school." Dorn smiled at me in an especially discomforting manner. His eyes were always beady and crooked. "So what you play then Cherry?"

"I was a centerfielder until my sophomore year." I picked up a golf ball sized rock and fired it hard from down on my knees. "I had a good arm and they needed another pitcher, so I ended up doing that for my last three years." Baseball didn't draw the attention that Ant's pussy stories did. Most of the guys were taking amongst themselves by then.

Ant said with intrigue, "A pitcher then Cherry? I'd a made you for a third baseman."

73

Dorn interrupted, "The hot corner, shit, what you thinking Ant? Cherry look like he can make that toss across the diamond? Maybe a two bagman."

I asked Dorn, "So, what did you play Specialist?" He looked back at me, as if I had stepped out of line by asking the question. We locked eyes for about a second and he finally responded, "Third."

"Baseball, fucking pussy ass sport that is."

"Amen Sergeant." SFC Holliday spoke in conversation very rarely, when he did, SSG Reynolds took it as an opportunity to agree. SFC Holliday was huge. He was black, and to me that made him more intimidating. His voice was deep and grumbly, and matched his husky tall frame and rough but handsome face. His expression was authoritative but kind. SFC Holliday preferred football.

"You played some college ball didn't you Sergeant?" SSG Reynolds knew he played college ball, everybody did except for me. "Played at UCLA for two years. Left to go to the Gulf." Apparently SFC Holliday was some football player back in the day, but his warrior spirit diverted him away from the football field and toward the battlefield. I couldn't have imagined him anywhere else, but I sometimes wondered if he could.

Sgt. Lyons threw a filled bag up at SSG Reynolds. "You put that ball in the squad box, right?" SSG Reynolds looked over at SFC Holliday and said, "Sure did Sgt. Lyons."

"Yo Lyons, Alpha versus Bravo man. Any time you want to." Sgt. Eden spoke for the first time, Valentine and

Dorn stopped what they were doing and looked at Sgt. Lyons with stoic glares. I noticed them both, then turned toward Sgt. Lyons and dubiously did the same. "WHAT THE FUCK ARE YOU LOOKING AT CHERRY? Get your fucking ass back in that fucking sandbag." My heart raced and I immediately regretted my fortitude. Sgt. Eden was unaffected by Sgt. Lyons' demeanor. "Let me know Lyons, Alpha's always ready."

Tolson perked up at talk of the contest, he started laughing hysterically. "Alpha, against bravo? Common Sgt. Eden. You and Valentine yeah, we all seen Dorn play ball though, Sergeant. He couldn't catch a batch of genital warts. And then you got the Cherry." Tolson looked over at me and winked; I returned a casual smile. Sgt. Eden came right back. "Hey man, like I said, whenever you want. Alpha's right here man, you know where we stay." Tolson dropped his half full bag and playfully but deliberately charged Sgt. Eden, taking both of them to the ground. With a smile on his face, Sgt. Eden skillfully rolled over so Tolson was on his back with him on top. The squad divided into two cheering sections, excited shouts and instruction boiled from both sides, "GRAB HIS ARM, PULL IT DOWN."

"HE'S GETTING TIRED, YOU GOT HIM."

"GET HIM TOLSON, GET HIM."

"YOU GOT THIS SEGREANT, HE'S A BUM."

Sgt. Lyons stood up and glared toward the crowd. SFC Holliday was enjoying the bout as much as anybody, and he always welcomed a random feet of strength. They went at it for about three minutes. Sgt. Eden finally was able to wedge his forearm between Tolson's chin and chest. It was all for fun, for esprit de corps, but the look in Sgt. Eden's eyes was all business as he applied the choke to Tolson's throat, slowly cutting his air supply until he finally tapped out. It was a good moment for alpha, a good moment for the whole squad really. And those were soon to be in short supply.

Valentine filled our bag to the top. I tied it off and turned to throw it toward SSG Reynolds. When I opened up another sandbag for Valentine, as I bent down to squat, I was halted. Somebody had a hold of my pants. I was shocked, but right away I knew that familiar feeling, it had been some time, but it is quite distinguishable. I was getting a wedgy. An infantryman learns quickly not to wear underwear. It gives you nothing but swamp crotch. But it makes it so you can really get that shit wedged up in your ass if you get caught slipping. I had a guy on each side. Sgt. Eden had my left side, and Dorn my right. They lifted me off the ground, at least two feet, and threw me down at the peak of their lift. It wasn't even my ass so much as it was my dick and my balls. The crotch of my pants served as a cradle to lift me well off the ground, and I had each testicle split between that rough seam as I became airborne. I hit the ground with considerable force, but the loose dirt of the pit absorbed the blow enough that I could extract the humor from the situation, although my dick felt like it was just split down the middle with a rusty butter-knife. The whole squad exploded with laughter as I was lifted from the ground. I think I even heard Sgt. Lyons in their somewhere.

"Alright, stop fucking around now. We gotta get these pits dug for the mortars." SFC Holliday was just enough business.

The rest of the squad was back to work, as Valentine patted me on the back and handed me the shovel and said, "Sorry man, squad traditions. Here you go, you dig for a while now." Once I pulled the better part of my pants from my ass, I started back to work. "Goddamn, I didn't see that shit coming. You guys get everybody like that?" Everybody laughed and Valentine looked over at Browning. "Tell him Brownie, nothing new is it?" Browning just shook his head. Valentine looked back at me and said with a grin, "We all get it Cherry. You'll get the next guy, watch."

Sgt. Eden asked whoever in the squad had an answer, "You ever heard them called Melvins?"

SSG Reynolds confusingly asked, "Melvins?"

"Yeah a Melvin, you ever heard a wedgy called a Melvin?" I had heard that when I was a kid somewhere.

"Yeah I have Sergeant, my dad used to call 'em Melvins."

"You know why they call it a Melvin anyway?" I didn't know, nobody knew. Browning offered up the best explanation, "I imagine the first person to fall victim to one was named Melvin. Just sounds like a dude who would get the world's first recorded wedgy doesn't it, M-e-l-v-i-n." The squad laughed together for the last time I can

77

remember.

FIRST CALL HOME

I was stressed. After about a month I tried to jerk off. Jerking off in a shitter made of plywood in the middle of a combat zone takes both resilience and determination. It's even worse in the summer when you add heat and sweat into an already foul scene. The cold of the winter made it a bit easier to handle the smell, and at least you didn't drip perspiration like a fat man in a hot dog eating contest. But in twenty-degree weather, the paratrooper finds another obstacle in which he must overcome, that is fishing three inches of winter dick through four inches of clothing. Once you managed to poke your cold shriveled cock through a layer of long underwear, polyporpaline bottoms, and dessert cammo pants, you had to grasp it with a filthy half frozen hand. With your free hand you had to hold the stroke mag while standing up, leaned against the side of the shitter to both stay as far away from the well of piss and shit as possible, and keep your rifle propped up against the side. There was no room for further distraction. The picture I had of my girlfriend that I carried in my wallet before was inside of my bullet proof vest. We didn't have any patrols for a couple of days, and the down time weighed on my mind. I missed her, not just fucking her, everything. I hadn't called her yet. If I hadn't accidently dropped her picture down into the shitter while fishing my dick out, I don't know when it would have been before I finally did.

"Hello."

"God your voice sounds good." It calmed my angst immediately.

"BABY, I miss you. How are you? Are you okay? Where are you? Why haven't you been able to call yet?"

"I'm good, we're good. I can't tell you where I am, but yeah I'm fine. I'm not going to be able to call you very much, maybe once a month."

"What? Why just once a month?" I wondered how many questions she would ask that I had a negative answer for.

"They only have one phone here, it's some kind of high speed satellite phone, or something. I guess it costs like ten bucks a minute or something."

"Once a month though, that's not fair. The army can afford it."

"Yeah I don't know. Hey, I can only talk for like ten minutes at a time though so…"

"Ten minutes? Ahhhh. Baby, I miss you so much."

"I miss you too. I love you, baby."

"I love you too."

"Baby I missed you so much on Christmas, I just cried all day." I didn't know how to respond, so I asked her, "What did your mom get you?"

"Clothes and stuff, you know. A purse I wanted. Did you guys at least get to celebrate with your platoon?"

"We were on a mission actually. We didn't even have orders for one is the fucked up thing. They figured that if we were just sitting around on Christmas we'd get depressed about being away from our families, so they sent us on a mission to occupy our idle time."

"That's not fair. They shouldn't make you guys do that. You should get Christmas like everybody else." She wasn't trying to, but she only made me feel further from home. "Well I'll be home next year babe."

"Baby, I need your address so I can write to you and send you a package."

"Oh yeah, you have a pen and paper? I got it written down."

"Yeah, go ahead."

"Okay, it's APO 96227 82nd Airborne Division 3/504 Parachute Infantry Regiment Alpha Co. 1st Platoon 1st squad."

"So APO 96227, and then your unit, all the way down to 1st squad?"

"Yep."

"I'm writing you a letter when we get done talking. And tomorrow, I'll send you a package."

"I love you babe."

"I love you, are you doing alright? What's it like?"

"Yeah, I'm fine, it's hard to breathe at this elevation, hiking up and down the mountains and shit, and there's no showers."

81

"It's hard to breathe?"

"Yeah, the elevation, we're like two miles up."

"Holy crap, two miles!"

"Ha ha ha ha, ahhhh, I love you so much baby."

"What, what'd I do?"

"You said crap, not fuck, not even shit, but crap. Like you're in fourth grade or something."

"Are you making fun?"

"No, I love it, I love you. And I miss you. It sucks not being with you."

"I hate not being with you."

"You gotta be getting kind of used to it by now though. I left for basic a while ago now, it's been awhile."

"I'll never get used to you being gone. Anyway, when you get back, I can start working on transferring over from University of Portland."

"You still want to do that?"

"What, move to North Carolina when you get back? Of course I do, it's all I think about every day, that and how much sex I'm going to have with you when you get back."

"Fuck babe, I miss you so much, I can't wait to be with you."

"How long are you guys suppose to be there, do you know yet?"

"Not really, I can't really say anything about that anyway."

"So, how is it?"

"It's cold right now, way cold. Yeah, I don't know."

"It's okay baby, I'm just happy to talk to you. I'm so

happy."

"Me too babe, but my times running out here, I gotta get off here in a minute."

"Nooooo, tell them you can't go. Tell them I said no."

"Cummon, don't make it any harder babe."

"I'm sorry, I know. I just…why do you have to be in the army?"

"Babe, common, you know I can't…"

"What, you can't what?"

"Babe, not this. Common now, you know I had to come here."

"You didn't have to." I was relieved to look at the phone and see my time was up. "Babe, I'm sorry, I have to get off now, the next guy is waiting."

"Noooo, just a few minutes."

"Babe, I can't. I have to go, there're people waiting in line. I can't be a dick. Sorry, I love you."

"I love you." The hesitation in her 'I love you' was enough at the time to render the sentence meaningless. In Afghanistan, there were no good calls home.

"I love you too. Bye babe, love you."

"I love you, bye."

"Bye."

SHOOT-MOVE-
COMMUNICATE-KILL

After a month in Gardez, I was disappointed that I hadn't gotten a kill. By that time I had already been fired at five times. All five attacks involved small arms fire (AK-47), and the last began with a rocket propelled grenade. We actually drew fire every night. It was always a show at night. About every fifth bullet is a tracer, so when rounds are fired by either side, tracer rounds are mixed in, which give off an illuminating glow that could be seen at night and trace where rounds were going, hence the term, 'tracers'. Coalition rounds always had red tracers. The rounds the enemy combatants had were always green, kind of like in Star Wars with the different colored light sabers, although we hardly wielded the Force. Anyway, it's quite easy to locate the origin of a series of rounds being fired. If we weren't taking random fire from the city to our south, it was coming from the mountains that faced us to our north. The exciting nights were when it was coming from both directions. I say 'exciting' without intent at irony, it was exciting. The risk factor of being hit by a round was almost zero. The firebase was just out of range of small arms fire from both the city and the mountains, so it was just slightly more dangerous than an indoor light show. It was actually quite beautiful. At two miles above sea level and without the obtrusive lights of a modern city, the green hazes would flash at you like short neon tubes in the backdrop of a million stars that are visible from few other places on Earth. Amidst all that chaos, the sky's allure was always in such a way as to instill you with a sense of calming insignificance.

I was waiting to drop the hammer on somebody. Being fired on is only a semi-exhilarating experience. I would say only slightly above a mild car accident. If you see your enemy before, during, or after the bullets come at you, it raises your adrenaline significantly. I had found that that usually was not the case though. Usually while on a patrol if you drew fire, you never knew exactly where it came from, unless they continued to fire, which they usually didn't. They weren't dumb. They realized that they could fire off a three round burst at soldiers without them pinning the origin. Anymore and they were had. But often that's how it would be. You would just be walking along, then BAM....BAM, BAM. And that would be all. You could pick up the general direction, but when you're out in the open hiking up and down mountains, it's nearly impossible to determine the distance, so you usually just took cover and waited around for another shot that never came. That was frustrating as shit. When you could see your enemy, they were so dug in and far away that confirming a kill was equally impossible. Most firefights began with complete confusion and ended with uncertainty at best.

I was still waiting to get that homerun pitch. That perfect shot when your target is at that ideal range so as to sit snugly between your sights, face to face, so you can see each other's eyes. Pretty fucked up as I look at it now, but that's what the army wanted. I don't give a fuck what they say, the army wants killers. Contrary to belief they don't try to dehumanize the enemy so the individual will look upon them as somehow less, subsequently making it morally easier to kill. I believe the opposite is true of the army's conditioning. True, racial terms are used. In Vietnam it was Gook, Slope, Slant, or Dink. We had Sandniggers, Towelheads, Abduls, and most commonly, Haji. That's just because people in the army are generally racist anyway, it's that simple. It has nothing to do with intended dehumanization. The army drove the opposite idea into my head. During basic training I said 'kill' fifty times a day. Whether we were running for morning PT, doing disciplinary pushups, or were just waiting in the chow line, we were chanting one thing or another about killing. Every step we took, 1...2...3...4...SHOOT...MOVE...COMMUNICATE... KILL. Every stop, ONE SHOT...ONE KILL...KILL WE WILL. There was no racial attachment. It was under no other context except in regard to killing a fellow human being. The army wants its infantryman to believe that they are invincible. If the soldier is to think that the enemy in which he is defeating is somehow naturally inferior to him, his virility diminishes. This sense that you are the toughest motherfucker on two legs, with or without a rifle, is what the army really tries to condition its men into thinking. Dehumanization used to be the name of the game when it came to getting human beings to be unconditionally ruthless against other human beings. During my generation, the army tapped into American Alpha-male idealization, a manifestation created through years of movies, advertising, and organized sports. When the army figured out how to tap into that, they really started producing some soldiers drooling to kill for their cause. I didn't think less of the Afghan people, some did, like Dorn, but he was a bigot anyway. I had every respect for my enemy as an equal, and therefore as a worthy adversary. That was the appeal, it's why I wanted to shoot and kill one of them so badly. That was the highest competition, to find another badass and to do the death waltz until one of you falls out. I was still waiting for my counterpart in that moment of complete black and white truth, between life and death. And for my sins, I got it.

SFC Holliday gave the briefing. The whole squad was going out as part of a larger regional mission. Our squad had a wet dream of an assignment. Intelligence handed reports down to Battalion about a neighboring village of Gardez supposedly providing food and shelter to the Taliban as they crossed the border between Afghanistan and Pakistan. The village was in a valley at the end of a bottleneck in the mountains, and I imagined just as old. The Charlie Co. platoon from Gardez was to enter the village from the bottleneck while our squad and two Delta Co. trucks provided security at the rear of the village. What made the mission so alluring to us was that we knew that when the villagers were alerted to Charlie Co.'s guys entering the area, they would likely gather all weapons and tactical vehicles and head for the rear of the village. The idea was that the villagers would be alarmed by our presence blocking off the rear of the village, and would be then likely to open fire and try to escape anyway. If this happened, they would be immediately shut down by a mixture of small arms fire from us, and blocked from escape by the .50 caliber machine gun and automatic grenade launcher from the Delta Co. trucks. It was as if we were flushing game. Charlie Co. was the golden retriever, and we were the fat white hunters in lawn chairs waiting for the game.

Just minutes after Charlie Co. approached, the villagers were already sending vehicles to the southern end where we were prepositioned for the planned counterassault. On the south side the village ended with a rapid incline in the land with a road running parallel against the valley wall. We had a Delta Co. truck positioned at both ends of the T-intersection, and our rifle squad was positioned straight away, about seventy meters up the valley wall. If the villagers tried to exit the village using the road, it would be blocked off by both trucks. The road bent slightly around the curvature of the village's perimeter, so the trucks were not directly in each other's line of fire. The idea was that the villagers would feel trapped and instead of trying to escape without going on the offensive, they would be forced to engage the trucks, at which time, we, from our advantageously elevated and covered position, could assault them with ease.

Seconds after the word came down on the net, SFC Holliday, positioned between the two fire teams, yelled out, "THEY'RE COMING THROUGH, THEY'VE GOT TRUCKS AND WEAPONS. DON'T OPEN UP UNTIL THEY FIRE A SHOT."

I remember thinking to myself, what if they don't fire shots, what if they just try to speed off in their vehicles, do we just open up on them anyway? I looked to my left and right and saw Sgt. Eden and Dorn. Sgt. Eden was kneeled down behind a tree just a couple of feet below me on the hill. I whispered to him. "Hey Sergeant. What the fuck, I can't even see anything." Houses along the backside of the village prevented blocked our view inside. We only had the radio reports and sounds from the village to inform us. Charlie Co. was sweeping through the houses starting at their end and working their way to the back very deliberately. They were to keep clearing the houses, and we were to recover any escaped villagers through the south end.

Finally three shots fired from an M-4 rifle rang above the screams and vehicle noises coming from the village. No shots were returned. SFC Holliday, with one ear in the radio, yelled out to the squad. "There's a truck headed for us that has a gun mounted in the bed. Get ready. Watch for a gunner and take out the vehicle." The loudening vehicle noise and the dust trail that hovered above the buildings hinted at the carnage to come.

Sgt. Eden looked up at Alpha team and said, "Alright boys, just like we were on the range back at Bragg."

A second after the first truck barreled around the corner straight away into our sights, another followed, and then another. There were dozens of villagers speeding along the convoy on foot, some appeared to have weapons, others certainly didn't. Had it not been for SSG Reynolds being positioned where he was, about four feet to my eight o'clock, I'd have never known who fired the first shot. I distinctly remember the feeling of the muzzle blast as it passed my neck and ear. There was no machine gun mounted in the first truck, just people piled in the bed, the same was true for the second and third trucks.

Everyone of them might as well of had a rifle in their hand, because out of the sixteen men that we slaughtered with small arms fire that day, three of them had AK-47's. I could tell you what the man who I shot looked like, but I still couldn't tell you whether or not he had one of those weapons or not, because the truth of the matter was that I didn't look. He was alongside the second truck, the first bunch that came through did not draw my fire, but as the second came through and I listened to the shots of my fellow squad members tearing through the air, I had to take part. I was a hundred feet from him. We were close enough to look into each other's eyes. His were deep and stoic. I still wonder what he saw in mine before he died.

That was it, it was bigger than my first homerun or

when I popped my first cherry. I wish that I could say that it was bitter sweet, but the truth is that I had never felt so pure and uninhibited in my life. The only thing that I detest more than my action on that day is the unbridled exhilaration that I experienced through its events. Nothing had ever felt so natural in my life as when I dropped the hammer on that random villager. The confused teenage angst I shared with the peers of my generation combusted with years of American alpha male conditioning and misguided patriotism, and it all at once released itself from the end of my rifle in twisted orgasmic bliss. At no time in my life has a more perfect manifestation of conditioned behavioral reaction taken over every bit of my natural consciousness than at that perfect moment that it all turned off, and I killed.

WALK IN THE PARK

All members of the squad were present, our weapons were cleaned, magazines were checked, water, all the shit for the mission was ready to go as we sat on our bunks waiting for the operation order. Routine patrols usually involved a fire team, four guys, with maybe a couple of additional personnel, so maybe you had six guys on a patrol, and they rarely lasted over three hours. This was a battalion level mission, which meant at least a couple of days, with the involvement of all battalion personnel in the area of operation; no reconnaissance, no hearts and minds, our orders were from Corp intelligence and were simple. I was still reverberating with barbarous egotism from the kill I got in the village a couple of weeks prior. I looked forward to the mission and anticipated it as an opportunity to amplify that feeling.

Sgt. Eden, Sgt. Lions, SSG Reynolds, SFC Holliday, and Lt. Youngblood from Delta Co. filed in the tent with

Sgt. Eden in the rear. As they each came in, they panned over the squad, each wearing their own signature expressions. Sgt. Eden remained standing, starting right away. "Alright, everybody knows that Lt. Youngblood's boys from the Delta section took out a high priority target two days ago in the Seti-Kandow Pass. Before I get into what's going on tomorrow, Lt. Youngblood's going to brief us more thoroughly on his mission in the pass. Lieutenant." Sgt. Eden took a knee next to Dorn who was sitting on his bunk, and as usual had his helmet already on, readily holding his weapon in both hands. Delta Co.'s Lieutenant was polished and stern, a real crusader. His red hair was cropped tight, and his cheeks were always red, either from the sun or from the cold.

"Alright guys, I've gotten to know most of you by now, and I just want to start by reiterating how well you all conducted yourselves in the village two weeks ago. Now I can't stress the importance of this mission enough. Just two days ago my first section received intelligence from some farmers who live along the pass that they were approached weekly by the Taliban and were receiving an increasing amount of pressure to take up arms against the American forces in the area. Now these guys don't want to side with the Taliban, remember that men. But we have to make sure they keep that freedom to make the decision for themselves. We were fortunate that last time while we were there a probe of Taliban forces came into the village. As soon as they saw our vehicles they began firing on us, all small arms fire. Our 50 cal. took out the six of them within seconds before they could disperse. At first we thought it was just another routine Taliban element trying to put pressure on the locals. It turned out that a few of these members had key intelligence, and the part you all probably heard, one of them was Farzan Sharif-Rahim. The guy is a major player". He paused and put his index finger in the air. "Well, the guy was a major player." A mix of hooahs, war cries, and growls roared toward the Lt. "We received intel that there would be a funeral held in a nearby village where he actually grew up. If the intel is sound, there should be other high profile targets in the area. Namely, we're hoping it will bring his brother. We should be able to take out whoever is in attendance with considerable ease, given the battle plan. This funeral is going to be held in a public area, should be like a park or something. So before I hand you over to Sgt. Eden, I want to stress women and children will be present at the funeral. Identify your targets men. Hooah." The Lieutenant took just one step to the side as Sgt. Eden got back up and took the floor, with the Lt. at his hip.

Sgt. Eden's operation order was brief and uncomplicated; it was a simple albeit important mission. Sgt. Eden would have kept it short and simple even if it wasn't. He always said that things were fucked up on the ground enough, no need to complicate it with shit you didn't even know about. Stick with the intel you have, and stay loose. Sgt. Eden's briefings made me feel more comfortable with the fact that I was an eighteen year old member of an airborne infantry element tasked with hunting down Bin Laden and friends and killing them. We were to work as a squad on the mission with the aid of two Delta company trucks armed with four men and a MK-19 automatic grenade launcher and .50 cal. machine gun respectively. We would be in a third vehicle positioned between the Delta trucks. All we could round up for the mission was an unarmored open bed humvee, so we'd be relying greatly on the cover of the Delta trucks, and we would be completely vulnerable to the blast of any improvised explosive device. Our interpreter Farid would accompany us as well, which made some of the squad very uncomfortable. I heard Dorn say to Ant, "Taking a sandnigger on a patrol to talk to the locals is one thing. Riding in the back of a truck with one is another." I trusted Farid and looked at him as an asset as both an interpreter and an additional set of watchful and weary eyes.

Farid quickly proved a reliable ally. His grasp of English was better than most in the squad's, and his upbringing had made him astute and enduring. After a month in Gardez, I'd been on almost a dozen patrols with Farid. On one of the first, he may likely have saved all of alpha team when he spotted what ended up being an improvised explosive device concealed in a dead animal carcass. We were on our way back from a routine patrol through the city. We had walked through the market on our way back to the firebase as part of our orders from above to mingle with the locals and to stimulate the local economy; part of the whole 'hearts and minds' motivation for our occupation. After buying some bread and other shit, Sgt. Eden had decided to patrol the main road through the city as a demonstration to the locals that they were safe from the Taliban while we were there. Still on the main road through the city, although still just a dirt one, Farid approached Valentine, who he was closest to in the formation.

Valentine halted the formation, calling for Sgt. Eden's attention. There was what looked like a dead goat about two hundred feet up the road. It was common for goats and other animals to be killed on that road, and the rest of us thought nothing of it. Farid said the animal looked too intact and that something was fucked up about the whole thing. The Taliban had adopted a caliber of guerilla warfare the army hadn't seen since fighting the Viet Cong. They would often slaughter a goat or other large animal, hollow it out and stuff it full of some simple explosives, usually left over from the war with the Soviets. They often had remote control fuses, so some dick holding a cell phone, or pager, or anything that will send a signal, would be hunkered down in some ditch, just out of the blast radius, patiently waiting for some American soldiers to come strolling by, then BOOM. Sgt. Eden had me fire a grenade round at the goat. The round landed about two feet from the goat, enough to roll it over and blow it to the side. A half second after my round landed, the goat exploded with a blast at least three times the force of my grenade round. Seconds later, a guy popped up from the ditch and sprinted away from us. Farid yelled for him to stop. When he didn't, Sgt. Eden put two rounds through his back. I guess Dorn was still unconvinced.

We drove for a day to get to the Pass. It wasn't far

but the mountainous terrain made any trek an excursion. SFC Holliday seemed to enjoy it the least. I loved riding in the truck in Afghanistan. And even more especially when the convoy was small like it was on that mission. There was something about the emotional opposition, riding slowly along rocky trails that bend around towering mountainous peaks on both sides. Looking up one felt like the smallest particle in the world, susceptible to any of nature's whims; but at the same time, as you creped along the canyon beds and caverned floors with an automatic rifle in your hands and an Airborne patch on your shoulder, you somehow felt in control of it all. The contrasting emotions created a sense of vigor so unadulterated as to convince me of my complete indestructibility. There was really nothing like it, and I'm glad I haven't felt it sense.

Every truck had a gunner with a crew served weapon. Our truck was not a traditional uparmored humvee like the ones Delta Company used. It didn't have additional battle armor, and it didn't have a gunner's turret built into the top. Ours was a cargo humvee. It was for transporting goods or troops, but not in a hostile fire zone, what the fuck those trucks were even doing in country I don't know. Valentine stood up in the bed with his SAW bipod extended and resting on the cab of the truck, while Tolson and Browning hung off the sides providing peripheral security. Every couple of minutes we'd hit a big bump and Ant or I would have to catch Valentine. We all chain smoked during the six hour drive.

Thanks to some intel, which we received by

administering various interrogation methods to one of the locals, we found out that the funeral services would not be held until later on in the evening, we didn't know when exactly, it was noon at the time. The main body stayed prepositioned about two miles from the suspected funeral sight. Sgt. Eden, Ant and I performed a stealth patrol so as not to allow the locals to know that American forces were in the area. The intel we received from the Lieutenant was sketch. The first sight we rolled up on didn't look right. Sgt. Eden showed no frustration as he confirmed our grid location. "Well, this is it, we're in the right spot, these are the grid coordinants right here. Yeah, there's no way though man, it's not here. I'm sure the Lt. was close though. Let's walk along the side here and see if we see anything. Stay down and keep quiet guys." Sgt. Eden led us along the perimeter of what was too small to be a village, and there weren't many houses. It seemed like maybe just a farming depot, like the one we made our firebase from in Gardez. The Lt. said it was going to be like a park, but this place didn't look like that all. There were about two dozen mud huts spread around sporadically and a few recently used fire pits. We watched from the trees, where we laid, as they were too small to provide cover to three standing men. Sgt. Eden scanned with his binoculars and spotted some movement. It was eerie. We watched a single man come from his mud shack, dragging behind him a large burlap bag filled with something, we couldn't tell what. He was older, his body looked not just skinny, but frail, yet his movements showed that he was still strong. He wore a cream turbine and a brown Shalwar kaeez. Sgt. Eden kept watching through the binoculars, but said nothing. We were close enough that Ant and I could see him fine, but far enough that our voices wouldn't carry. "What's this fuckn' guy doing, where the fuck is this funeral? Where the fuck, is everybody else? Sergeant, this ain't it, we're in the wrong spot."

"Just shut up for a minute Ant." Sgt. Eden's voice said that he agreed, but he had a wandering tone. The man dumped the contents of the bag onto the ground in the middle of a rock ring. He tossed a liquid on the pile, then a match, and we watched as the flames roared up above his head. The man took a couple of steps back and sat down with his knees on the ground and began moving up and down from the ground in prayer. It didn't make any sense, and I was beginning to grow uneasy, which Ant already was. "What the fuck you think he's doing Sergeant?" Sgt. Eden remained silent. I knew he heard me, but he just kept watching him through the binos like we were at a ball game. He dropped them from his eyes, and put them in his pack. "Alright, this is what we're going to do. I don't know what the fuck is going on with this guy. And I can't see anybody else around. You guys see anybody else?" I answered with a head shake and Ant said, "Ain't shit here Sergeant, don't make sense."

"No it doesn't, but it doesn't need to. There's nobody else here and this guy has his head up his ass. This funeral must be going down close by here. Ant, I want you to stay here and provide security for us. You'll be by yourself, so watch your six. We're going to sneak around these huts and snag this guy up. You should be able to keep a watch on us the whole time. Once we snag this guy up, we're going to disappear into one of those huts. If everything is cool, we'll be right back."

I didn't know what to make of Sgt. Eden's plan, "What are we going to do Sergeant?"

"We're going to snag this guy up while Ant covers us. Now stay low and follow me." I started to crawl on my stomach toward the first hut in a series of four leading up to the unsuspecting man.

"Wait wait, Sergeant, what are we going to do with him I mean?"

"See what he knows. See if we can find out where this fucking funeral is, Harris."

"How we going to ask him Sergeant, we need Farid, we should have brought Farid."

"Come on, we don't need the interpreter, he'll know what we mean." I didn't feel confident about the plan at first, but Sgt. Eden's bold determination always helped.

The man was still in prayer with his back turned to our position. The wind and roar of the fire muffled our soft footsteps to a silence. We stopped just feet away from him behind a hut. I looked back at Ant who put a hand in the air as to indicate that he could see us. Whispering I said, "Sergeant, Ant's still got us in the woodline." He was visible only because I knew his position.

Sgt. Eden whispered back, "Good. Okay, I'm going to hug the side of this hut and make sure it's clear, stay right on my ass. I'll peak in, and if it's clear, come off me, you just bum rush this guy and pull him right in. Got it?"

"Yeah I got Sergeant. I couldn't fucking believe it, I was going to actually grab this guy with my fucking hands.

"You ready for this? You got this right? You got this."

"I got this Sergeant, I got this."

I thought 'Oh shit, why couldn't I have just stayed in the woodline'. Sgt. Eden began to move to the front of the hut, the whole time hugged against the side. The man was still in prayer, and now chanting. As Sgt. Eden got closer to the front of the hut, the chants got louder, and the fire roared higher and hotter. Half of Sgt. Eden's body disappeared as he wrapped himself around the corner. I expected a signal immediately, but there was some hesitation. Just as I was about to tap him on the back, his right arm swiftly jetted out in a downward cutting motion to the side and I peeled off him like a halfback dashing out from behind his blockers. The man was only about six paces away, but still didn't hear my footsteps plowing toward him. I noticed just then for the first time, the AK-47 that lay on a blanket to his side. I thought that he would jump up immediately but he didn't, and instead, his first notice of my presence came to him when I wrapped my right arm around his neck and swiftly brought him back and onto his feet. My arm cut into his neck, muffling whatever words he was uttering into mere gurgles. I remember the way he smelled, like fire and spice, and the way his wiry hair felt on my face and neck as I held him as tightly as I could.

101

At the time I thought that I was as scared as he was.

Sgt. Eden kicked him in the back of the knee, bringing him hard to the ground. He kicked his ribs, turning him over on his stomach. All at once Sgt. Eden slammed his knee into his back and ripped his arms back and together behind him, forcing the flex cuffs onto his wrists, the man then screamed. "COVER HIS FUCKING MOUTH, NOW GODAMMIT." I moved fast, but my hands shook with adrenaline. I ripped open my first aid kit and stuffed the Afghani's mouth with a bandage. I slammed him in the nose with my fist, sending blood immediately from both nostrils. He continued to wither and resist until Sgt. Eden slammed his boot down on his face and into the rocky ground. He stuck the tip of his barrel into his eye socket. "Get that cravat around his head and eyes and stand that motherfucker up." My throat burned from breathing so fast. The smoke of the fire hued the scene with a grayish fog.

"Sergeant, we need Farid, we should have Ant get on the radio and get Farid up here."

"We're the goddamn scouting element, the main body's two miles away. We'd give away our position. The three of us stood in the hut. Sgt. Eden in front of the bleeding Afghani whose head was wrapped in my cravat and mouth stuffed with a bandage, and me holding his flex cuffed arms from the rear. Not one of the three of us had any idea as what to do.

"Okay, put you rifle to the back of his head so that he can feel it pressed against him. Then pull off the cravat.

If he starts going crazy, crack him in the back of the head."
I let go of the cuffs, sending his hands to fall freely. I
jabbed him in the small of his back with my barrel and
slowly dragged it up his back and stopped at the middle of
his head. As my barrel stopped, I could feel the pressure of
his head pushing back against it. He didn't turn his head, or
step back, forward, or to the side. He was perfectly still.
He just stood there pressing his head back into the anxious
barrel of my rifle. I didn't want anything to happen. I
wanted him to speak English somehow, and to know when
and where the funeral was. I was angry when he didn't.
Not at him, but at the situation, that it always seemed to get
worse. We yelled at him for a couple of minutes like angry
American tourists who were lost in the German subway.
Violations of noise discipline all around by this time. I
don't know if he understood anything we asked, probably
some. Sgt. Eden pointed to his watch and made various
other gestures in a modest effort to communicate, but he
remained still and silent. Sgt. Eden became frustrated after
pointing to his watch, asking him 'when, when', over and
over. He threw him against the wall of the hut and walked
outside. "Stay here, get what you can out of him, I'm gonna
get the radio from Ant. We can get Farid on the other end
to ask this fucker what's up." Sgt. Eden walked outside the
open door, he picked up the man's rifle and released the
magazine onto the ground and walked out of our sights. I
wonder now if the man was relived or scared as Sgt. Eden
left us alone.

I knew that Sgt. Eden didn't expect me to get

anything out of him. I didn't know what he expected. I knew that he'd be gone for at least five minutes though. The Afghani, who was probably forty, although it's often hard to tell, was small, but strong. He didn't stand back up when Sgt. Eden through him against the wall, and he was then staring up at me from his knees, not with any scowl, just a blank face. He didn't look like he wanted to attack me, nor did he look scared. I stood there in the hut, maybe six feet in front of him, and raised my barrel to point between his eyes. His stoic expression remained. I looked deep into his eyes and unsnapped my chin strap, letting it swing freely, I said to him in anger, "You know what the fuck we're asking you, don't you? How 'bout it Abdul, where's that fucking funeral at, where's it at, huh?" His head dropped to the side and he looked around the hut, which was no bigger than a high school baseball dugout. I stepped forward. Planting my boot square in his chest, I kicked him to the ground. "LOOK AT ME WHEN I TALK TO YOU MOTHERFUCKER." Our eyes were then fixed on each other. He was again on both knees, and remained unaffected. He came slowly to one knee and as he began to stand up, my left hand came off of my rifle and right into his mouth. As my fist hit him I could feel a mix of tissue, nose, lips, teeth, gums, and tongue on my bare knuckles. With his hands cuffed behind his back, he landed with full force onto his face, splattering teeth and blood across the ground like a Jackson Pollack painting. I dropped my weapon, letting it hang tightly to my body form its combat sling. Grabbing him by his collar with both hands, I lifted him with force enough to bring him off his feet. I kept a hold of his collar with my left hand and brought my right hand back as far as it could reach, and then forward, slamming it into his mouth a second time. Barely conscious as his head came back forward, that stoic look remained, and I hit him again, and then again. His eyes were closed, his face mashed, covered in blood and dirt. I dropped him to the ground. I wasn't enraged; I wasn't out of it. There was a great void. At that moment I felt nothing.

Sgt. Eden came back with the radio to me standing blankly above the unconscious Afghani man. "What the fuck man? What the fuck happened, what'd he do?"

"He just kept coming closer and closer to me. I told him to back up, but he kept coming at me. I pushed him back and then he came at me and grabbed by barrel, so I cracked him."

"He's all fucked up man, you knocked him out. For fuck sake, he's still alive isn't he? What the fuck did you do Harris?" I had no idea if he was still alive.

"Yeah he's alive Sergeant. I just punched him a couple of times." Sergeant Eden got on the radio telling Sgt. Lyons on the other end to hang on for a few minutes. He went over to the man to roll him from his side over to his back, when he pushed him over, his bloody face spilled with coagulated blood.

"Fuck Harris. What the fuck man, you knocked some of his fucking teeth out. He's all fucked up. He's not going to tell us shit man. Goddamn it Harris, you could have just cracked him once for fuck sake, this guys weighs like a hundred pounds. What the fuck got into you?"

"Sorry, I lost it for a bit Sergeant, he grabbed my barrel, and I…I just reacted too aggressively, fuck, I'm sorry." The apology was only to Sgt. Eden, I was sorry only as far as it affected the mission.

"Fucking A you fucked up man. We're supposed to be getting intel from this guy. This is an important fucking mission, man. This isn't like you man, what the fuck Harris?"

Sergeant Eden poured water from his canteen into a cravat and began cleaning the dried blood and dirt from the man's face. He was kneeled next to him. Holding him, he took off his helmet and looked up at me as I remained standing and gave a slight shake of his head. I thought less about what I had just done and more about how I still had the inability to feel remorse or empathy regarding it. My anger was not directed at this man, it wasn't at the high priority target that Delta Company got, nor was it at the one that we would get later that day. The man regained consciousness minutes later, terrified. He pissed himself and divulged everything we needed to know to Farid without further coercion or threat. Sgt. Eden's disappointment faded into relief and surprise when the information he gave ended up being the exact intel we needed to execute the mission. I didn't get to take part in the actual assault to take him down, but I was later recognized as the soldier responsible for "retrieving the necessary intelligence to make the success of the mission possible." A week later, I received an Army Commendation Medal for my actions on the mission.

ANOTHER CALL HOME

"Hello?"

"Hey."

"Baby?"

"Yeah babe, it's me."

"Oh my god, oh my god, baby, I miss you so much. Ahhh I miss you so badly."

"I miss you too."

"Are you okay, are you guys doing alright? Oh my god, I'm so glad you're calling, I was so worried. It's been almost a month."

"Yeah, sorry, babe, we've been pretty busy out here, and there's just one satellite phone for over fifty guys, so, you know, it's hard to get a chance to call. I miss you though. I can't wait to see you."

"I can't wait to see you baby.

"How are things back home? How are you?"

"Things are fine here. I stopped by your house the

other day. Your mom wasn't home, she was out shopping with your grandma, but your dad was there and we actually talked for a few minutes."

"You talked to my dad? I mean my dad talked to you?"

"Yeah, he did, he was actually in a really good mood. He was sitting on your deck drinking a Coke and reading a paperback. He seemed like he was actually glad to see me." He wasn't, he may have been being polite, but my dad was never glad to see anybody.

"Yeah I'm sure he was. My dad likes you. You know, as much as he likes anybody. Yeah, he always thought that you were good for me, that you brought out my best."

"He said that to you?"

"No, course not. Can you imagine my father ever speaking those words, or anything that even resembled them? No, I could just tell. When he heard your name he didn't just ignore it or wrinkle his nose. If I told him I was going to go out or meet up with you, he would always pleasantly inquire. You know him though, that's more approval than he's ever given anybody." There were a few moments of silence, which I didn't mind. I was soothed by the sound of her breathing into the phone. "He loves you, you know that right."

"Oh yeah, yeah, yeah I know. How's school babe?"

"Um, okay, I actually ended up dropping my classes this semester. I just need some time adjusting to moving out, and I have to figure out my work schedule and stuff."

"But you were already enrolled weren't you?"

"Yeah, but, oh, baby I didn't even tell you, I met this really nice guy who got me a job as a hostess at the Montage."

"So you had to drop your classes?"

"Yeah but I'll only have to work three nights a week, so when I get my schedule figured out, I'll be able to work around school a lot easier than I could working at the nursing home. And besides, if I work there, I can start bartending as soon as I'm twenty-one."

"Bartending? Twenty-one? That's more than two years from now. I thought that you wanted to be a nurse."

"Baby I thought you'd be happy that I found a good job that I like."

"I am, but you had a job that you liked, and it was related to your field too. I just don't see how becoming a bartender is going to help you out as a nurse."

"That'll be two years from now, if it happens it all."

"I thought that's why you took the job though?"

"Because why?"

"So that you could eventually bartend."

"No, that's just an option down the line, I took the job because it frees up my schedule better for school."

"Babe, you had to drop your classes to take this job, how the fuck is that more conducive for school?"

"I haven't gotten to talk to you for a month, and I don't know when I'll get to again. Can we just not argue about this, I just want to hear about how you're doing."

"I'm fine, you don't need to worry about me.

Who's this guy who hooked you up with this hostess job?"
I could hear her sigh, but her voice remained the same.

"Oh he's just some guy that Tera knows form
school. He bartends at some bar next to campus I guess."

"So how's he going to get you this hostess gig at the
Montage?"

"Well he's a bartender, you know how it is."

"No, I don't actually, how the fuck would I know."

"Don't be like that, I know you must be stressed
but…"

"No, no, no, no. How's he just getting you this job,
and I thought you were moving here anyway?"

"I am. What is wrong with you? He knows the
bartenders and manager there, they needed a hostess, and
he told 'em about me. Baby, he did it for me as a favor.
And it's just a way to make some more money before I
move there."

"And what's he getting out of it?"

"Joe, are you serious? I'm not going to have this
conversation with you right now."

"When then? You know where the fuck I am? You
have any fucking idea what I'm doing out here, what I have
to think about all day? And you're telling me you can't have
this conversation."

"Joe, I can't do this with you right now."

"Why not, why, what do you have going on that's so
fucking important? I've got a mission to go do. You know
what the fuck happened on the last one? You even know
what's going on over here? No, none of you fucking people

do, six months after 9/11 you stopped giving a shit. You're comfortable, you have your fucking bars, and your fucking college, and hostess jobs—WHILE I'M FUCKING STUCK HERE."

"I never wanted you to go. You didn't give a shit though Joe. I told you, you just signed up anyway, then you just left. What about me, what about how I felt? You asked, and then you just went ahead and left anyway. You didn't give a shit about me. Now you're going to pull this bullshit?"

"Yeah I'm going to pull this bullshit. How many fucking letters have I gotten from you, or fucking care packages. Valentine and some of these guys get a couple of letters a week from their wives and girlfriends, they send them food and magazines in packages. You haven't sent me shit, I haven't even gotten a fucking letter. I'm on your mind, you worry about me—BULL FUCKING SHIT. You don't give two shits what happens out here."

"Joe, I have to go, I have to get ready for work."

"I thought you didn't even have a fucking job right now. You don't have class, obviously. What the fuck do you have to go do all of a sudden?"

"Stay safe, bye Joe."

"NO, this is bullshit, GODDAMNIT DON'T FUCKING HANG UP ON ME."

"I'm sorry, I have to go Joe."

"SAM."

"Bye."

"FUUUUUCK."

Joseph Andrew Holsworth

ALL ALONG THE WATCHTOWER

We had a nasty blizzard come through the pass and dump four feet of snow on us overnight. The weight of the snow had caved the roof in on our northern guard tower. So until the next day when it could be properly repaired, whoever had guard in north tower would be in the turret and on the hood of a parked humvee in front of the only gate to the firebase. Having only one tower from which we had a three hundred-sixty degree view also left us considerably more vulnerable. Sgt. Lyons and I had a two-hour block together from 0300 to 0500. We got up as a squad at 0600, so you didn't have time to go back to sleep really, it was the asshole of guard shifts.

The first hour went by in almost complete silence. In light of Sgt. Lyons' less than loquacious tendencies, I didn't expect much in the line of conversation. I guess it's not fair to label him as reserved, in just the two months that

I had known him, I could recall at least eight incidents in which he chewed a soldier apart, top to bottom, for minutes without taking a breath. He had laid into Tolson just days before. Bravo team was doing a routine recon patrol around the perimeter of the village. It was all good out there, but when we got back he tore Tolson's asshole right out from underneath him.

Sgt. Eden thought it wise to have an additional SAW (squad automatic weapon) gunner for fire support if we are going to be going on these long daily patrols, one of the first deviations from the standard practice of our usually rigid infantry tactics. So now when Bravo team went on a patrol Dorn or I would take Valentine's SAW. Likewise when Alpha team went out we brought along Brownie or Ant with Tolson's weapon. The beauty of the SAW gunner is that he requires no assistant gunner to carry his ammunition or maintain his weapon as it is being fired. The proficient SAW gunner operates individually as an "automatic rifleman", with the range and accuracy of a rifleman and the fire rate of a crew served machine gunner. I had already learned of Tolson's reputation as an ace with the SAW, and that day I witnessed it for myself. Sgt. Lyons was less impressed.

On these patrols, we usually travelled in a standard wedge. The standard wedge consists of three soldiers in a straight forty-five degree line with a fourth soldier alongside and parallel with the second soldier in line. So from a bird's eye view, the soldiers form an uneven wedge that looks exactly like an upside down check mark. The formation revolves around the SAW, with the team leader in front, the SAW gunner behind him, the grenadier to the SAW gunner's side, and a rifleman behind him. As advised by Sgt. Eden, an additional SAW gunner, a fifth team member, trails the formation providing rear security and additional fire support.

We were on our may back to the post, not too far out, and a vehicle approached us going the opposite direction. We all stopped and took fire positions as a precaution, however it was a common dirt trail that was often used by farmers in the area, and we had not yet been fired upon by a single one. It was a small rusty gray pickup truck with two men in the front. It slowed only slightly as it passed us; every weapon in the team was fixed upon their heads. I was the rear SAW gunner, the last man in the formation. As the vehicle passed me, it slowed down slightly before stopping suddenly, maybe two hundred feet past me. I immediately extended the bipod of my SAW and dropped to the ground in the prone firing position. I could hear Sgt. Lyons behind me yelling at the squad to, "STAY ON BOTH THOSE MOTHERFUCKERS," and at Tolson to, "COVER THE REST OF THE FORMATION, WE GOT IT IN THE BACK." I was nervous but not shaken up, and the excitement that I felt that first time in the village was now significantly diluted. I thought about them pulling a weapon from their truck and opening up on them, the whole team opening up on them with everything we had. It would be right in front of me like a big screen at the cinema. They didn't even get out of their vehicle. They just stopped as the dust from their break swirled around them in a scattered haze. You could barely make out the backs of both men's heads. I yelled up to the front. "THEY'RE STILL JUST IN THE VEHICLE SEGEAT."

"FIRE A WARNING SHOT NEAR THEIR VEHICLE."

As my finger steadied down on the trigger, I was startled by the sudden burst of three rounds. With my eyes still fixed on the truck, I saw a burst on the side of the vehicle where the rear view mirror once was, followed by a dust trail where the truck used to be. I heard Tolson yell, "YEAH MOTHERFUCKER, YOU SEE THAT SHIT!"

Watching the truck as it grew dimmer in the dust and in the distance, Ant came running down to my position to get a cigarette from me. "What the fuck Cherry? You know you gotta be quicker than that with my man T on the gun. Almost some crazy shit went down. Let's get the fuck on out of here Cherry." I lit one for myself and returned the bolt of my weapon to its neutral forward position.

As we returned to the firebase, I thought about what would have happened if I had opened up on that truck. Not if they had gotten out with a weapon. I thought about what it would have been like if I had just shot them as they sat in their vehicle. As soon as I would have pulled my trigger, the rest of the patrol would have followed. Nobody would have known who fired that first shot. Nobody would have cared. The men in that truck only stopped for an instance as they passed, but had I been of a different mind, they could have shared the fate of those villagers.

I thought of Tolson's shot. A second after the command came down from Sgt. Lyons, with a single burst, he blew the mirror clean off. It wasn't so much the shot, but his readiness that had me still in awe. I was fixed on them. I had them pegged and had every intention of pulling the trigger on them upon seeing any upper body gesture that I could constitute as an "aggressive movement," but Tolson was really ready. I had lost that part of me by then. I was strangely hesitant.

I don't know if Sgt. Lyons might have let it go if it were not for the gloating and prattling that went on back in the tent. Sgt. Lyons went to report the suspicious activity of the truck to SFC Holliday. I went right over to my bunk in order to return a cleaned weapon back to Valentine as soon as possible where both he and Sgt. Eden were asleep on their backs with field jackets over their heads. SSG Reynolds, Van Dorn, Sgt. Tell and Doc Evans were directly across from me. They were playing poker at our card table made from a piece of plywood sitting atop a square formation made of two bunks. The players sat on extra gas tanks. SSG Reynolds asked me, "Anything worth telling?"

Just as I was about to respond with I don't know what, Ant chimed in with, "Fuck yeah Sergeant, you should have seen this shit. We was just walking back and one of those little shit haji trucks comes rolling up on us. It fuckn' up and stops as it gets to the end of the wedge. Sgt. Lyons says to give a warning shot and Tolson's like a hundred meters out and blows the fuckn' side mirror right off, BAM, fuckn' in pieces. Fuck'n truck peels off down the fuckin' road. You shoulda seen that fuckn'shot Sergeant, with a fuck'n SAW." Before the impressed faces at the table had time to say anything regarding the account, Sgt. Lyons came roaring in and threw his helmet across the card table, scattering chips and tobacco spit bottles across the tent. As SSG Reynolds got up in a hasty reaction to Sgt. Lyons, whatever he had to say was postponed by what Sgt. Lyons had to say right then.

"SHUT THE FUCK UP. Nothing happened on that fucking patrol except for Tolson not following fucking orders. You think that shit's impressive, Ant? Firing whenever the fuck you feel like, at whatever the fuck you feel like. I DIDN'T TELL TOLSON TO FIRE. I TOLD THE FUCKING CHERRY TO FIRE. But I guess we do what the fuck we want, don't we Bravo team. Come back here and fucking gloat to Staff Sergeant Reynolds about some shit that was all kinds of fucked up. Fucking idiot! And Ant, since Tolson's going to be busy for the next twenty four hours and you got such a fucking hard-on for him, you can pull his guard shift tonight."

All the smiles in the room had melted into flat lips, none more than Ant's. He answered as somberly as I ever heard him. "Roger Sergeant."

"Well get fucking going Ant. I think it's time for you to go relieve whoever the fuck is on the truck right now in fact." Ant grabbed his gear and moved slowly for the door. Sgt. Lyons kicked over Ant's bunk and yelled out, "MOVE MOTHERFUCKER." He mad dogged Ant his whole way out before turning his attention to Tolson.

119

"GET YOUR SKINNY ASS THE FUCK OUT HERE SPECIALIST." Sgt. Lyons tossed his weapon on his bunk, tore off his vest, and threw it toward the ground nearby. Tolson ran out the tent behind him. While SSG Reynolds silently went over to Sgt. Lyons' area, he carefully placed all his gear on his bunk in an ordered manner and returned to the make shift poker table to do the same. Well within earshot Sgt. Lyons tore into Tolson with the contempt of an ex-wife.

"I'M GONNA BEAT YOU WITH YOUR OWN NUTSACK—YOU SKINNY ASS LITTLE FUCK STICK! Now get the fuck on your face and start pushing. I don't know who in the sweet shit you think you are, but this is my motherfucking team. BRAVO FUCKING TEAM LEADER, right here motherfucker, not you, you little fucking sack of squirrel shit, this is my fucking team, and you better get on fucking board. YOU FUCKING GOT ME SPECIALIST?"

"Roger Sergeant, I..." A thud that sounded curiously like one paratrooper throwing another to the ground could be heard loudly from inside the tent.

"SHUT THE FUCK UP MOTHERFUCKER, DON'T SAY ONE MORE GODAMN WORD OR I'M GOING TO STOMP YOUR FUCKING HEAD INTO THE GROUND. YOU FUCKING PIECE OF SHIT." By this time everyone in the tent had stopped acting like they didn't hear what was going on and we were all looking back and forth at one another. SSG Reynolds kept his head down and looked at his cards while the rest of us silently mouthed things back and forth to each other. Sgt. Lyons went on like that for another ten minutes. If nothing else, his endurance for things like this intimidated us all. A strange jealousy overtook me. I hadn't known Sgt. Lyons enough to be deemed worthy of him exasperating himself in my face with every ounce of hatred and despondence he could reach for. But if Sgt. Lyons took the time to shred you apart it meant two things, that you fucked up and were going to hear about it at an unreasonably high volume for an unreasonably long time, and that you were worth a shit enough for him to muster up that seemingly ever-flowing hatred of his.

Last week when I pulled guard with Sgt. Lyons, his only words were repeated twice in the shift, 'Do a radio-check with tower two.' That night would have been no different had it not been for my foolish loquaciousness. Aside from a radio check, the first hour had gone by in complete silence. I thought of my girlfriend, Samantha. Not about fucking her, like I had a month before, just her face, I just pictured it in my mind. I worried about our last conversation, and how it ended with her hanging up. I had confounded my mind with worries of Dear John letters, a letter which I probably deserved after our last talk. I had to talk. Guard was usually a great time for that. If you talked about mundane bullshit, you didn't have to think. I didn't like having time to think.

Ten minutes into our second hour, as cold as it was, my palms were sweaty with angst as I thought about my Samantha. The risk of angering Sgt. Lyons by speaking to him seemed diminutive compared to the distress that my silent ponderings were creating. Against my better judgment, I spoke. "Where is it that you're from Sergeant, I heard Pittsburgh?" His countenance remained, and without opening his mouth, a quick sigh came from his nose, the breath making a visible swirl in the frigid morning air.

He answered, "Pittsburgh, who'd you hear that from?"

"I can't remember who Sergeant, it was my first day here, somebody told me then I think."

"Didn't take long to hear about me, did it Cherry?"

"Well, what do you mean Sergeant?"

"You know what the fuck I mean. That I'm an asshole, to watch out for me and shit like that."

"No it wasn't really like that. I mean yeah, you know how it is, guys talk, but it was more that you were just a hard ass, a bit more by the book than some of the other sergeants is all."

"Cherry, I don't give a fuck alright, don't worry. I'm not here to make fucking friends. See that's the difference between Sgt. Eden and me. I'm here to do my job. My job is to lead a rifle team. I want my men tactically proficient and unquestionably obedient. I don't give a fuck if they like me or even respect me. But they will respect my rank, my position, and my authority. And I'm not from fucking Pittsburgh Cherry, I'm from goddamn Philadelphia."

"Philly? Where did I get Pittsburgh from?"

"Well I'm a Steelers fan. I wear my shit when I'm off work a lot. Everyone just assumes I'm from

Pittsburgh."

"Well if you're from Philadelphia, how in the hell did you become a Steelers fan, seems like blasphemy in that city?"

"I liked to piss people off." He smiled. It wasn't the first time I had seen it, but this one was at me. He let out a light chuckle. I wanted to keep talking.

"Yeah, I'm a Seahawks fan, hardcore, I…"

He cut me right off. "Just scan your sector Cherry, alright." I felt worse than before. Another ten minutes or so went by in silence. I gave another radio check. "Hey Cherry, just do radio checks at the top of the hour, roger?"

"Roger sergeant." And that was it for another twenty minutes. I couldn't fucking believe it. How the fuck was this guy married? And then it happened.

"Who do you think is the best quarterback of all time Cherry?"

As stunned as I was, I didn't want to show it at all, and tried to answer very quickly, "You probably want me to say Terry Bradshaw, but I can't do that Sergeant."

"No. I was never about Bradshaw, guy's too fucking stupid. You hear as a fucking commentator? Guy's a blonde version of Ant for fuck sake."

"No shit Sergeant, he does remind me of Ant. Fuck yeah."

"So Cherry, who do you think? Best QB ever?"

"Okay yeah, let's see here. If I'm going to be completely objective and say the best quarterback of all time…"

"Well, that's the fucking question Cherry, so, who the fuck you got?"

"Johnny Unitas then Sergeant, no question."

"Get the fuck outta here Cherry. Johnny fucking Unitas?"

"1958 Super Bowl Sergeant, 'Greatest Game Ever Played.'"

"Fucking 1958 Cherry? How fucking old are you?"

"I'm eighteen, but I know my NFL history. And we're talking all time here, Sergeant. Johnny Unitas is your man, no fucking question about it."

"Fuck that noise Cherry. The league was way different back then. Those guys would never last in today's game."

"You can't say that Sergeant. That's like saying that Babe Ruth was just really good because the pitchers didn't throw as hard. Bunch of fucking bullshit. You can honestly sit there and tell me Sergeant, that players that thrived in past eras in sports, don't measure up to today's athletes?"

"What I'm fucking saying, Cherry, is that Johnny Unitas would get his crew cut ass sacked every fucking snap going against a modern day D-line."

"Okay then, who do you got then Sergeant?"

"Best? I don't really know, hard to say."

"Oh what the fuck Sergeant, you just chew my ass down for saying Johnny Unitas, then you're gonna give me an answer like that, common Sergeant."

"Alright Cherry, you're right, you're right. Lead by example, hoooah. I gotta go with Marino."

"Kind of pussy Sergeant, I gotta say."

"What the fuck Cherry? Pussy? Dan Marino? I'll pull you outta that fucking turret right now."

"Alright Sergeant. Alright. I'm not saying that Dan Marino is a pussy, I'm saying that your selection is pussy, it's too safe Sergeant. See, Dan Marino is a good choice, but that's the thing, statistically he is almost unarguably the best, so it's too easy to shut down an argument by just throwing out his numerous records. He's too easy to defend. It's a pussy selection Sergeant." I think it was my repeated use of the word pussy that did it.

Sgt. Lyons cut me right off. "Give me that fucking radio Cherry." With his expression returned completely to its normal self, I reluctantly handed him the radio. "Now get out of the turret, put your weapon down here on the hood with me, and get into the front leaning rest position." I didn't regret beginning the conversation with Sgt. Lyons. I did however at that moment look upon him with more despondence than ever before. I felt so quickly betrayed. For a few minutes we were able to rise above our time and place and just be two guys talking about football. I hated him so much for snapping us both back to our painful reality.

I LOVE THE SMELL OF BURNING SHIT IN THE MORNING

IT SMELLS LIKE DEMOCRACY

It was my day to burn shit. We rotated, which is to say that the privates rotated. Each of the makeshift shitters had cut off oil drums in the bottom. About every other day these two feet wide by two feet deep shit canisters needed to be emptied. Since there was no viable area in which we could dispose of the waste, our only option was to consume it by fire. Add a dash of diesel fuel to the mix, toss on a lit match, and keep it stirring. It eventually forms a melting-flaming stew of boiling feces which very slowly turns to a blackish smoke, most of which passed through the respiratory system of the private stirring the pot, and you have got to keep stirring the pot, otherwise it just goes out.

I ended up burning shit about once a week. Aside from the assumed unpleasantness of inhaling the burning fumes of excrement from over fifty soldiers, this detail was not as bad as you might think. The shit was on fire, which kept you kind of warm in the blistering morning cold of the Hindu Kush. There was the added unpleasantness of the smoke residue that inevitably clung to whatever it touched, up to and including the paratrooper's face. The thing to do was just enjoy the solitude and the heat and block from your mind the fact that the blackish resin covering you was reminisce of burning feces. It was nothing that a couple of baby wipes couldn't take care of.

Burning shit gave a guy time to think. I thought of back home. I didn't think about what was going on though. I thought mostly about change. How I had, and the world probably hadn't. I wondered how I would fit in to it. I was more estranged from my upper middle class upbringing than ever before. I never fit the mold and my choice to join the airborne instead of going to college was seen as youthful irrationality at best. They had their degrees, and their houses, and their boats, and their bullshit, but they had no stories. The ones they had were pedestrian at best. White middle class stories of potato salad and waterskiing.

A couple days before, I had received a letter from my mom and dad with some new family pictures from Christmas. There was a copy of their Christmas card in it too. As an only child, my mother especially, felt it necessary to parade me around in the trendiest and most expensive of toddler garb throughout my youth. Now that I was gone, it was the dogs. The fucking card had her two dogs with Santa and elf costumes on respectively. She was from a middle class family and had a two-year-older brother. She had owned her second Corvette at twenty-five, bought the four thousand square foot house that I grew up in at thirty, and retired just after fifty. She used to tell me about the real world, and how rough it was to make it. She was right, but how she acquired that understanding through her experiences was beyond me.

My dad was no better. While he was the only one to give me any real support for my decision to join the army, he was the one who should have forbidden my enlistment above anybody. My dad was the only person other than my grandfather who had ever worked for the federal government in any capacity. My family loved America because it supported their materialistic lifestyle. They unquestionably supported the government because they were the governing body of the hierarchal system in which they found themselves toward the top of. But my father should have known better. He was an air traffic controller all through the seventies and up until 1981. My father was actually a harbinger of the air traffic controller's strike of 1981. When working conditions and safety standards were diminishing due to operating procedures allocated by the Federal Aviation Administration, the union decided to strike. Ronald Reagan effectively ended the strike by firing all union members involved. It was a wake-up call to the working American to not fuck around with The Man. He didn't protest, he didn't rebel, he just wrote letter after letter apologizing and begging for his job back. As a child I came to learn of the incident as an irrational rebellion of my father's professional youth which he had regretted every day forward. He tried to work for the post office afterward, but found that he and his fellow union strikers were turned away from all federal employment following their termination. He still always said to me, "go government, they pay you the best, and after twenty years you can retire, I wish I'd have done things differently son." My parents were like most of the baby boomers and would have worked for the Gestapo if they had a good enough medical plan.

I was relieved when I saw Farid approach, as I wouldn't have to be alone with my rigid thoughts. As the weeks in Gardez passed, I became increasingly judgmental toward any lifestyle that didn't lead people to the bullshit I had to deal with. Farid dealt with the same bulllshit that I did, and I appreciated that about him. And after he saved our asses on one of our first patrols, I showed him that appreciation by treating him somewhere between the enemy I was fighting and a low ranking private. While I enjoyed our talks, I thought of myself as charitable for forming anything beyond the cold relationship he had with the rest of the guys.

Everyday he wore the same boots, pants, and shirt, and if it wasn't dark, his eyes were shrouded by his Oakley A-frames. His beard and mustache were as black as his glasses, and the beanie he wore over his head made him look like a cat burglar, he looked really cool. I think Farid wanted to look cool. At the time, I foolishly thought that Farid wanted this war too. He came to me after morning prayer.

"Harris, what's up my main man? Thought you burned shit last time, what gives my man?"

"Fucking Sgt. Lyons. It's not Browning's fault, but fuck man, every fucking time it's his turn, Sgt. Lyons sticks him on some other bullshit detail, just so I'll have to burn the shit again."

"All you guys don't like Sgt. Lyons, yeah?"

"No, he's pretty much a dick."

"He's good leader though, yeah?"

"Yeah, I guess so."

"Sgt. Lyons is a good leader. Sgt. Lyons is a good man."

"He's pretty cool with you?"

"He's kind, more than any other of the sergeants I worked with." Sgt. Lyons was a dick and I didn't see how Farid saw it any differently.

I kind of snapped back with my response, "What does he talk to you about."

"He doesn't really, not much."

"Why do you think he's so nice then, man?" Farid wasn't elated as he usually was, and had been when we had started the conversation. He was a little sad.

"He's helped me. He helps me every few days." I had no idea what that meant. Farid went on patrol with Sgt. Lyons plenty, but all he did on patrol was yell and be an asshole too, so I didn't know what the fuck Farid could be seeing that nobody else did.

"What do you mean man, like when you guys do your patrols, what does he do?"

He sighed and shook his head, and for the first time responded to me with hints of temperament. "No Harris, no. He helps me and I help him too. All you guys have me pick you up cigarettes and things at the market, but he always pays me back." Farid was the guy everybody went to for shit like that.

"What do you mean? When you grab guys smokes and shit they don't pay you back?"

"Not usually, and it's okay, my friend gives them to me as favor. He knows I work for you guys and he likes America's soldiers. But Sgt. Lyons, he always gives me money when you guys forget to. I tell him I wouldn't take it at first but he made me, he always gives it to me since. He said to me, 'give it to your friend if you don't need it.' Sgt. Lyons is good man." Sgt. Lyons was still a fucking asshole. Farid's story did little to adjust my stance on that topic.

I really just didn't want to hear anything else good about him so I ended it with a succeeding smile and, "I guess so man. Hey man, that reminds me, I'm not going to be down town for a few days, can you grab me a few packs of smokes, I don't have any money on me, my shit's in the tent, but I'll get you back."

Farid nodded his head in compliance and quirked the corner of his mouth at the amazement of my aloofness, and asked, "Want three?"

"Yeah man, three would be good."

"Don't worry about money. But Harris, can you get me something else you think?"

"That depends, man, what are you trying to get?"

"The porno, you can get me the porno?"

"Porn, you want some porn, like a porn mag?"

"Yes Harris, yes. You can get me the porno then?"

"Yeah man, I can get you a porn mag. We have tons."

"I know, I see you guys carrying them around sometimes."

"Yeah, up to the guard towers and shit. Yeah man, Valentine's wife, she's fucking cool. She sends him a package like every two weeks. They always have shit for the whole platoon. Best thing, she always sends five or six new Hustlers or Penthouses. Yeah man, I'll just grab you one of the old ones that nobody really looks at anymore. You might have to clean the jizz off some of the pages but they'll be good."

"Very much Harris, I thank you very much."

"Yeah it's hard for you guys to get porn here right, the whole Muslim thing?"

"Yes, yes, Islam says no porno."

"You're a pretty hardcore Muslim though, aren't you Farid?"

"Hardcore?"

"I mean like, you're a real strict follower of Islam and shit right?"

"I love Allah, and I follow his word the best I can. But I'm not strict about anything, not even Islam. That's why I don't join the Taliban. They try to recruit me. They recruit two of my brothers. But with the Taliban, there is no choice. I believe that we must always have a choice, Harris."

"So that's why you help us then?"

"I help the American's because you fight the Taliban. Before you came the Taliban were in charge, and there was no choice, you do what they say."

"Yeah, and the Twin Towers man, that was pretty fucked up right?"

"As a Muslim it hurt me that my brothers could do that. But America makes it a religious matter when it's not about that."

"What do you mean man? It's you guys with the Jihad, the fucking holy war." As soon as I said it, Farid's face turned. I'd likened him to the perpetrators of 9/11.

"NO. Not our holy war. You, America makes it a holy war. You say that Muslims start holy war, that they hate all Jews and Christians. That they hate Americans. Muslims just want their own land. We just want America away from our homes. America says, 'democracy' but they just want to build McDonalds and sell us Nikes."

"You don't want us here then Farid, is that what's up?"

"No, I want America. That's why I work for you. I want America, but only now. We need to fight the Taliban and we need help from America. But after, America must leave the Middle East. This is Muslim land, this is our land, and we will fight for it like we always have."

"What do you mean Farid? You say that America needs to get out of the Mideast, but in the same breath, you talk about how you need us to defeat the Taliban, I mean, what the fuck dude?"

"America created the Taliban, Harris. Harris, you're smart, think. American bases in the Middle East force the Taliban. Why you think they attack the Towers?"

"They're in New York, they were full of civilians."

"No, the Towers were a sign."

"What do you mean the Towers are a sign?"

"A sign, a sign, they mean something…something else. They're a sign for…" Farid's grievance began to slow his translation.

"Oh like a symbol? Yeah, you mean the Towers were a symbol. Yeah, yeah they were."

"Yes, yes, symbol, yes symbol."

"Well yeah man, I get that."

"The symbol though, what is that symbol for then, Harris? You say you understand."

"I don't know, they're just, or they were, just symbolic for America I guess."

"American democracy though, and your business, American business. Your capitalism. Your American Capitalism is what makes this war. Same as before you, in Vietnam."

"American Capitalism?" I knew what both words meant but didn't understand the implications of their pairing.

"Yes, that is it. American capitalism. America says

it wants to bring democracy, but they just want to sell stuff, they want their companies put here, they want our oil." Farid wasn't upset as he said all this. I listened while I stirred the burning shit pot. You have to keep stirring the shit while it burns, keep the air circulating. Farid sat squatting like a catcher on top of a small berm just a couple of feet to my side. He just wanted to survive, and at that time, we were his best avenue to longevity and prosperity, so he helped us. Within him though, he harbored a deep resentment. Farid hated the oppressive regime of the Taliban, and he hated America for fucking with Muslims in the Middle East, but he also understood that the enemy of his enemy was his ally. I think that as much as Farid resented the Taliban for their oppression, and the U.S. for its occupation, he resented himself for succumbing to either side. Farid was like my father in that he chose security and preservation over pride and principle. Maybe they were right.

"Not here though man, the Taliban brought us here, America was never in Afghanistan before 9/11." Farid didn't want to continue like this, I wasn't his enemy, even if I was making him mine. And it was good that we stopped, because I didn't have one fucking clue about the facts regarding my cemented convictions.

"Harris, I like you. I have no problem."

"No, I know, I'm just saying man, a lot of guys joined up to help you guys out man."

"Come on Harris. Soldiers don't fight to help people unless they're country wants something from those people. You want to help us, yes. But help us with what, by giving us your democracy? You want a government that does what America wants, America does not give a damn about our people, about Muslims. They don't give a damn about you, Harris."

"About me?"

"About you, Harris. They don't care about you. They want you to do a mission. They give you just enough to make you do that mission, just enough water, just enough food, just enough bullets. Why you think it's so hard for you guys out here? It's not like this in Kandahar, they have phones, and the internet, and Burger King. And they also have cameras. That's where CNN is, in Kandahar, not in Gardez, not here, Harris. The army builds stuff for those soldiers because they're on TV. Nobody sees you guys out here, so they don't care how you live. You're a number. They don't care about your life, only the mission. They treat us the same, Harris." I couldn't understand Farid, not just because I was young and stupid, but because he was right, they did treat us the same. I couldn't see that America was fucking over Muslims, just like I couldn't see that it was fucking me over too.

We were abruptly halted by three shots fired from the southern end of the firebase. Immediately after, the machine gun in the south tower opened up with continuous fire, and the screams of, 'AMBUSH' passed through the firebase. I started to run for my tent when Farid yelled, "HARRIS, YOUR RIFLE." I stopped in my tracks and Farid was standing behind me with my weapon in his hands and my mouth dropped. He held it toward me and yelled over the gunfire, "HARRIS, HERE, YOUR RIFLE." I grabbed it from him and we sprinted across the firebase to the bunker built next to our tent. The squad was already formed, and Sgt. Eden had my vest and helmet with him to put on. "Thanks Sergeant. What's going on, where's it coming from?" He calmly answered, "South side, I think we're headed down there now."

Just then SFC Holliday yelled, "LET'S GO, LINE FORMATION, ALPHA THEN BRAVO, LOCK AND LOAD, FOLLOW ME." SFC Holliday took off like a captain leading his team out of the Super Bowl tunnel. Firebase Gardez was under attack.

We built the hescos too close to the south guard tower, right against it if fact. If somebody were to escape the field of fire from the south tower, and were able to get right up against the outside of the hescos, they would be almost directly underneath the guard tower, and hence out of its field of fire. This proved to be a fatal flaw of the firebase.

Browning and Private Showalter were in the south tower when three vehicles, traveling north toward the firebase diverged off the dirt road and drove straight for the tower. Three shots were fired from one of the vehicles before Browning opened up on the approaching convoy with the 240-B. While he disabled two of the vehicles, the third escaped his fire and crashed into the hescos at the base of the tower. That's about when we showed up on the scene.

As the hescos blocked the direct fire from outside of the firebase, we could not return fire, nor could we tell what the hell was going on beyond the perimeter. Browning and Showalter were then firing at the men who had dismounted the disabled vehicles. The men on the ground returned fire and we watched above as rounds started to hit the tower where our brothers were then trapped. Sgt. Lyons yelled up to Browning, but with all the machine gun fire, they couldn't hear us. We could tell that they were both still alive because we could hear the distinct sounds of both an M-4 rifle and a 240-B machine gun respectively. Sgt. Lyons pulled two hand grenades from his vest, pulled the pins and tossed them just over the hescos. He ran for the ladder when SSG Reynolds grabbed and pulled him down by the back of his belt. Sgt. Lyons, yelled, "GET THE FUCK OFF ME REYNOLDS, MY MAN IS IN THAT TOWER." He kicked back like a mule and knocked SSG Reynolds to the ground. As soon as he was high enough to be within the enemy's field of fire, the ladder was shot to pieces. Sgt. Lyons stopped, took one step down and reached for another grenade. He threw another, which afterward caused a break in the enemy's fire.

Sgt. Eden yelled up at the tower, "ARE YOU GUYS HIT, GET DOWN OUT OF THERE NOW, GET DOWN." None of us caught what Browning began to say when the rocket hit the tower, sending debris and Sgt. Lyons alike down to the ground. Doc Evans pulled Sgt. Lyons back from the grenade struck tower. Sgt. Eden yelled out, "ALPHA TEAM ON THE HESCOS, OPEN UP,

NOW". I took a look up at the smoking tower, and a glance back at Doc Evans working on Sgt. Lyons, and time seemed to stop. I came to and Dorn was climbing up the wall while Sgt. Eden and Valentine were already firing down on the enemy. What was left of Bravo team ran to the opposite side of the tower, and began firing down from on top of the hescos. "Cease Fire" was yelled for at least a minute before the last shot was fired. Sgt. Lyons was temporarily knocked unconscious, and SFC Holliday's neck was broken from a piece of falling debris, the rocket propelled grenade killed both Showalter and Browning.

PART III
GOD HATES THE INFANTRY

TWO MORE WEEKS

It came over the net, "Tower 2, this is Tower 1 over." Valentine reached for the radio, "Go ahead 1."

"Roger 2, the 81's are going to be doing a live fire here in a few minutes, so be advised, roger?"

"Yeah, Roger that 1. Just, show of force?"

"Roger that 2. The two tubes are dropping twelve rounds a piece. Remind the locals that we got some big guns."

"Roger, when are they firing, over?"

"Should be in just a few minutes. They'll be rushing out of their tent like it's a reaction to contact, so be advised, just a show of force.

"Roger that, 2 out."

"1 out."

It was routine at Firebase Gardez, as it was with the rest of the Firebases, to quite regularly drop a series of high explosive mortar rounds at any given target as a kind of demonstration of our capabilities. These "show of force" fire missions occurred weekly at Gardez and were routinely fired at one of three peaks on the ridge-line to our and the city's north. There was a particular peak that ran just beyond the prevalent three, just as high but a half a mile or so further back. This fourth peak had never been fired on only because it was at the very limit of the range of fire for the 81mm mortar system, 6,490 yards. They're called 81's because they fire a round that is 81mm in diameter, or 3.2 inches across. The 81's wanted to show that they could hit the peak with enough fire power to make a visual difference at the tip. They got permission from battalion to dump a twenty-four round fire for effect at the top.

These fire missions were always a kick in the ass to watch; any time you drop a couple hundred pounds of composition B on something, it's a show. But with losing Browning and Showalter, it was an especially relieving distraction from the monotony of guard.

It was just three days after the attack when we got two pieces of news that brought a semblance of cheer to the diminished squad. SFC Holliday was supposed to make a full recovery. He would have a lot of rehabilitation ahead of him, but he would be back to running the platoon by the time we got back to Bragg. To be honest, I didn't think we needed SFC Holliday. I didn't feel as though we were without leadership in his absence, but this positive information about his eventual recovery brought me piece of mind for another reason. While for me Sgt. Eden was chief, SFC Holliday's mere presence was powerful and imposing. To be simple, SFC Holliday just looked like a warrior. He exuded badass. For him to be taken out of the game so easily, not even by a bullet, was disconcerting for us all. That he was going to at least live to fight another day was a small relief in a desolate bind.

The second piece of good news was that we were scheduled to leave Firebase Gardez in two weeks. It was the only place we had known for the last three and a half months, and the last place that Browning ever knew. Two weeks they told us. I'll call it a full two weeks. The horrific vividness in which my first three months in Gardez were recollected, has prepared me to write about the last.

With SFC Holliday out for the rest of the tour, and Browning dead, our strength and morale were diminished significantly. SSG Reynolds would move up to take over the platoon, which left a void in the squad leader position. With little resistance from Sgt. Eden, Sgt. Lyons moved up to take full control of the squad, leaving his team leader position open. Tolson took over as Bravo team leader by request of Sgt. Lyons. Valentine moved to Bravo team to take over as SAW gunner. Ant got the M203 that was attached to Browning's M-4 and took over as both rifleman and grenadier. With Valentine going to Bravo, Dorn took over the SAW. That left me bringing up the rear as dual rifleman and grenadier. We operated a man light on each team.

After losing Browning and SFC Holliday in the attack, we still did our daily patrols. Lt. Youngblood had his guys pick up our tower shifts when we were on mission.

South tower was rebuilt one hour after Showalter and Browning's lifeless bodies were carried down. Aside from the reinforcement of a dozen additional sandbags, the construction was exactly the same. The change in the base came with the reconstruction of the hescos. The attack was more strategic than sporadic, as was initially assumed. The three vehicles drove in a straight line convoy on the road running through the city and past the firebase. But when they broke off the road and directly at South tower, they split off into a staggered formation and gunned the gas. They turned off at the last minute, so as not to arouse additional attention from the tower, as the road was used often by farmers and villagers alike. From the road to the hescos at the base of the tower it was only a couple hundred yards, so it took less than ten seconds for the vehicles to reach it. Browning and Showalter were able to disable two of the vehicles with mere small arms fire, but the third got through, slamming into the hescos almost directly underneath the tower, thusly disabling their counterattack. Browning and Showalter were well occupied by the enemy fire coming from the dismounted troops from the two disabled vehicles. We could not directly engage any of the enemy troops as the hescos also provided them cover. By the time we overcame them with grenades and eventually scaled the wall in attack, they had already killed both Browning and Showalter with the RPG round. They took two of our brothers and just as disconcerting, they instilled within us a constant apprehension by exploiting an unbeknownst vulnerability. We all anticipated at what would come next.

Sgt. Eden had the aptitude to adjust our setup. The enabling factor in the attack was that the hescos were built too close to the tower, right up against it if fact. Elevation is a usual advantage; however, in that the tower was much larger at the top than at the base, shots could not be fired at a direct angle down at a target. The field of fire was reduced to targets extending about thirty yards out from the base; so if you got right underneath, there was no defense. Sgt. Eden suggested that we tear down that particular section of the perimeter, and take some of the extra empty hescos that the engineers left, and extend the perimeter out fifty yards or so.

I remember how empty I was during that time. I felt extremely vulnerable, we all did. We had lost men from inside the wire. All the pop shots, all the mile off target RPG's that we used to watch as late night entertainment from the towers were through. Every round and every grenade that came at us was sure to land right in our laps. It took twenty hours for forty men using only E-tools and our bare hands to extend the perimeter. That day, Valentine and I had first shift in South tower.

There were pieces of the wall missing everywhere. Some spots were full of bullet holes, in others you could see large chunks that were blown off when the RPG hit. The blood spots on the brown clay walls looked like splatters of dark brown paint. I never saw the bodies, but one of the walls had a blood splatter pattern that resembled a modern art canvas painting. The ground was covered with new sandbags that blocked the horrific effect that I'm sure was left on the ground. My pulse quickened and throat tightened as I ascended the latter. Halfway up my nostrils were already filled with the scent of a tomb. It smelled like burnt blood and carbon smoke.

"Tower 2, this is Tower 1, come in over."

"This is 1."

"Roger, be advised, the mortars should be coming out in the next two minutes. Twenty-four round fire for effect, over."

"Roger 1 out."

Out from the mortar tent rushed a dozen men toward their 81mm systems. Four men went to each tube, dug in circular pits twenty five feet wide and three feet deep and spaced about thirty yards apart. The four remaining soldiers stood in the middle with binoculars, radio, and two mortar ballistic computers respectively. The command 'hang it' came down from the Lt. who stood between the two tubes. A private from each team placed the mortar round three quarters of the way down the tube, holding it in place at the very top. On the second command of 'fire', the privates simultaneously released the rounds, sending them down the tube onto the firing pin, and back out at seven hundred feet per second. In one fluid motion the privates dropped the rounds down the tube, curling their body away from the muzzle blast while bending down to grab another round, which was handed to them by their ammo bearers. As the exchanges took place, the privates were on their way up to drop another round and repeat the process, twelve times, from each tube. Nothing could be heard for thirty seconds but the blasts of what sounded like old pirate cannons, their ringing bouncing back and forth around the valley walls. The noise was tremendous. Just as the last round was being dropped from each tube, the reports from the rounds were reported both visually and audibly on the targeted peak. The first few rounds landed right on the tip, as the rounds followed they trailed closer to the base of the peaks.

When the dust and debris settled after a minute, there was definitely a visible difference in the terrain. What was jagged on one side, was now jagged and uneven on the other, and slightly shorter, there were also a few small fires trailing down the mountain where some of the shorter rounds had landed and caught the vegetation on fire. The mortarmen were hooting and hollering like high school football players after a touchdown pass, none more than their Lt. As he jumped up and down like a school girl, the binoculars that hung from his neck bounced around his chest. Admittedly though, I enjoyed the show as much as anybody. And with the week we had, it was a welcome spectacle. From my post, I watched as the mortarmen smoked cigarettes and bullshitted with our guys and Charlie Co. I couldn't hear what they said to each other, but I could read the smiles on their faces as a welcome change. I think that fire mission did something a little different for everybody. For Valentine and me, it was a little less time we had to think about Browining. For the mortars, it brought praise. And that praise came from everybody. Because for at least that moment, we all felt like Firebase Gardez belonged to the 82nd Airborne.

Valentine and I spent the next thirty minutes or so playing the movie game, a favorite of Browning's.

"Sylvester Stallone? Okay Sylvester Stallone and Sharon Stone, the movie is The Specialist." I nodded in approval of Valentine's pick, and was amused by thoughts of Sharon Stone pleasuring herself on a red velvet duvet—a circa '92 Sharon Stone.

"Nice, fucking A. That movie's the tits. I haven't seen it in like six years. Okay, okay, Sharon Stone and Tom Berenger, and the movie is…" I paused to do a drum roll, turning to the blood covered wall and beating my fist against what once belonged to by brothers, I'm snapped right back to the reality in which they were dead. "Sliver." Valentine tipped his helmet back on his head and lifted his chin in suspicious examination.

"Sliver? I never heard of any movie named "Sliver". When did it come out?"

"Early '90s. Yeah dude, it's legit, I promise. Sharon Stone gets naked like a hundred times, it's sweet."

"Yeah, that is pretty sweet, but still, I'm going to need some confirmation on that one. Unless you want to go with something else."

"Not that I couldn't come up with virtually every movie in Sharon's filmogrophy to throw at you, but no dude, I'm sticking with "Sliver"."

"Fine man, but you know the rules, name somebody else in it, or you're sunk."

"Easy, Steven Baldwin."

"No shit? I don't know man, that's too easy. You just throw out a Baldwin brother as a co-star in a 90s flick, you automatically have a twenty-five percent chance. Those motherfuckers were in every goddamn thing back then. I'm gonna need confirmation on this one, Harris."

"Fine, not a problem." I looked at Valentine and we exchanged smiles, a transaction that rarely occurred at these times. I reached for the radio. "Tower 1, this is Tower 2, radio check over.

Dorn's southern twang answered back, "Tower 2, this is Tower 1, that's a good copy over."

"Roger, good copy. You ever heard of a movie named Sliver with Tom Berenger and Sharon Stone? Over."

"Roger that. Fuck yeah. My old man had that shit on VHS. Berenger's some kind of pervert watches Sharon Stone get fucked on his hidden cameras. Used to jerk off to that shit. Over"

"Roger, that's the one, I got Valentine here..." Valentine grabbed the radio from my hand."

"Tower 1, this is Tower 2 over."

"Go ahead Two. Who else was in it?"

"Ummm, one of the Baldwins...Billy Baldwin's in it. The best of the Baldwins, over."

"Roger, Two out."

"One out." My stomach sunk. I mixed up Steve and Billy. "Fuck, he's right it is Billy. Fuck, why did I think Steven?"

"Whatever, you're done. That's game."

"No fuck that, you gotta close me out man. You gotta name three more."

"Yeah? Three more with Sharon Stone? "

"Yeah, you can't name The Specialist or Sliver though. And you have to name somebody else in the movies."

"Name somebody else, what the fuck are you talking about? Since when do you have to name somebody else?" This was never a rule. I had to come up with a story and quick, and did. "Dude, Browning changed it man. It was too easy to close people out. We added that so the games would go longer."

"Bullshit Harris, I'm not buying it."

"Ask Sgt. Eden man, it was him and Browning who were playing when he came up with it." I knew if he asked I was fucked.

"No it's a good rule, I like it. I don't know about implementing it right now, when it happens to keep you alive, but for the sake of making time go by, I'll play along. So three additional movies with Sharon Stone, and I have to name somebody else in all of three them?"

"Yeah, otherwise we keep going."

"Alright, alright, I don't have her career catalogue at home like you apparently, but I can come up with three." Valentine always kept his chin strap snapped on guard, but he let it go and hang down. He pushed his helmet back on his head and scratched his forehead. "Let's see.." I gave him no time, "Let's hear it man, common then."

"Alright, "Basic Instinct" with Michael Douglas."

"Okay, that's one."

""Casino", De Niro."

"Nice, yeah I forget she's in that. Keeps her shit on the whole time."

"Yeah, that's gotta be like the only movie that she doesn't get completely naked in."

"Okay, one more man."

"I got one, I know I got one." I looked anxiously at Valentine. I wasn't worried about losing, but of having to bring my mind back to the incident in the tower.

"OH, "ACTION JACKSON", ACTION FUCKING JACKSON. She was what's his name's wife in Action Jackson. Bam, that's it, got you." I was impressed with the name drop of "Action Jackson", but I needed another name, I shook my head and said, "Yeah, with who. Who was with her in it?"

"You know the main dude. You've seen "Action Jackson", Harris, I know you have."

"Indeed. But have you? If you have, I would expect you to know the name of the lead actor. If you haven't, then I guess you can't name her co-star and you don't win."

"Harris, it's that same fucking guy from Predator, fucking Dillon. And fucking Apollo Creed. You know who the fuck I'm talking about."

"I need a name."

"Ahhhhh, bullshit."

"I need a name Valentine." Valentine took off his

helmet, laying it next to the 240B, he thought hard for a moment and a smile covered his face as it came to him. "Weathers, Carl Fucking Weathers. You're done. Got you. Action Fucking Jackson with Carl Fucking Weathers. "

"Fuck, fuck, fuck. Alright Valentine. It's only because I fucked up on that Steven Baldwin thing."

"Whatever dude. One lemon poppy seed pound-cake for me."

"If that's what I get." Valentine wasn't having it though, "No, bullshit dude. The rule is winner chooses his desired MRE item and it's up to the loser to get it for him. You're not just going to throw me whatever dessert is in your next meal. That's fucking bullshit. You're going to get a 'pasta with vegetables' whether you want it or not, because that's where that shit's at, and because you lost and you owe me a lemon poppy seed fucking pound-cake, now, Harris."

"Fine dude, whatever, I like 'pasta with vegetables' anyway man."

"Then I guess we both win Harris."

"Guess so man."

Our game was over. What came next kept Browning's loss at a distance for a bit longer, and it would later become the source of a whole new anguish. He just beat me, it was the first time anybody had done that. I probed for a rematch.

"So, how's the wife man?"

"Watch it Harris."

"No, I'm serious man, come on, you know I wouldn't…" Valentine looked me up and down and smiled.

"She's good man." Putting his head down and shaking it softly back and forth. "God I miss her man."

"You know I wouldn't say anything like that man. You never really get pissed though when the guys talk shit."

"No, Harris, I don't. You can't. This is the army man, the fucking airborne—ain't no sanctuary out here man."

"It's fucked up though. I mean most of those guys, like fucking Dorn, they don't give a fuck about their wives, so to them it's all good. That motherfucker thinks he can say whatever he wants about my girlfriend, about your wife. Fuck him man."

"It's just how Dorn is with everybody."

"Fuck all that though. I should punch that motherfucker in the mouth next time he says something about my girlfriend." Valentine looked at me, shook his head, and put his helmet back on, this time leaving the strap hanging.

"Well fucking do it then, Harris, or don't. I really don't give a fuck, just shut the fuck up about it and hand me those binos there." Valentine had never talked to me like that before. As I stared at him, not waiting, just stunned, he remained silent. He faced away from me looking toward the impact area, just holding his hand out toward me, waiting for the binoculars.

"HARRIS. THE BINOS, QUICK MAN." I pulled them from around my neck and instead of placing them in his hand, I punched them against his chest. Thinking nothing of my forceful gesture, he quickly took them and

153

put them up to his face.

I was put off, but my curiosity was peaked so I asked, "What is it man, what do you got?"

He didn't answer right away. "I don't know man. Somebody's coming toward the base. I think it's a kid. Way the fuck out there." Still fixed toward the mountains, without dropping the binos from his face, Valentine reached out with his free hand, pointing toward his area of suspicion. I could see the single figure making its way through a break in the mountain's base. It was too far to see but I remember the figure growing larger and less fuzzy.

"I can't really tell, is he coming toward us?"

"Yeah, something's up though. Looks like he's staggering back and forth or something, he's all wobbly. Looks like he's drunk. Get Sgt. Eden on the horn."

"Ranger 1 Alpha, this is Tower 2, over."

"This is Ranger 1 Alpha, go ahead 2."

"Roger, we got a single subject approaching the tower, about a thousand yards out, over."

"Roger 2, is he armed?"

I took the radio from away from my mouth. "Hey Valentine, you see a weapon man?"

"Hell no Harris, this dude is fucked up. Just tell him to come up here, alright."

"Ranger 1 Alpha, your presence is requested at Tower 2, over."

"Dammit Tower 2, is he armed, over?"

"Negative, negative 1 Alpha, the subject is unarmed, over."

"I'll be right there 2, 1 Alpha out." Valentine took the radio from me and handed me the binoculars.

"Yo, Harris, I think he's hit or something, he's holding his side." I looked up through the binos and saw the kid clearly enough to see him favoring his side with a large blood soaked cloth.

Valentine got on the radio, "Ranger 1 Alpha, this is 2. Come in over."

"I'll be right there 2, but go ahead."

Valentine put down the radio next to the M240B and turned toward the back of the tower where Sgt. Eden was coming up on the base of the ladder. He yelled down at him from up top.

"It's some kid, a villager or something. He's hit I think, he's fucked up. Get Doc Evans, the kid's almost at the perimeter between us and tower 1. They should be able to see him too." Without saying anything back, Sgt. Eden turned and ran back toward the tent. Valentine came back, grabbed the binos and looked back at the kid.

I asked him, "What's he doing?"

"I don't know, he's just waving back and forth. He's trying to get our attention. THAT'S IT MAN. He just wants help." Valentine let the binos hang from his chest as he vigorously waved both hands back and forth, trying desperately to signal to the kid that we saw him. The kid had a large bloody blanket around his side. His chest was bare. He wore ripped gray pants and no shoes. He was maybe ten.

Two trucks left the gate and went around the

perimeter to meet the boy. They came up fast in assault position, stopping abruptly and dismounting fifty meters back from him. Valentine looked over at me, "What the fuck are they doing? Where the fuck is Doc? What the fuck, the kid doesn't even have a weapon." Valentine held his hands up to his mouth and yelled out, "HE'S JUST WOUNDED, NO WEAPON, HE DOESN'T HAVE A WEAPON." Dismounted and walking deliberately toward the boy with their weapons fixed, they didn't respond to Valentine's shouts.

I could make out that it was Lt. Youngblood with Farid in the front and I turned toward Valentine and said, "What the fuck are they doing Val?" He didn't say anything back until in a moment of eureka he suddenly said, "Oh shit," and as I saw the boy pull the blood soaked material from his side. The Lt. and his dismounts took him down like a firing squad. Such a common word, every time I hear 'no' at a high volume, I watch over again, that small boy being blown apart and I can still feel the vibrations of that single word scream.

It turned out that the boy was from a small farm whose existence at the base of the mortar target zone was apparently unbeknownst to us. Lt. Youngblood and his men thought that the cloth hid a weapon that he was then reaching for, so subsequently, they filled him with multiple bursts of 5.556mm rounds. As he had no weapon, he was actually pulling away the cloth to let him know that he was no threat. I suppose he thought that by exposing the bloody cavity left in his side from one of the mortar rounds we just fired at him and his entire family, that we would assume him a non-combatant. He was the only survivor from our mortar fire mission out of his family of seven. After he dragged himself from the destruction of the blast area, he had the fortitude to walk in the direction of the shot. I guess he figured that if he made it to the base we would provide him with medical attention.

ONE TOKE OVER THE LINE

By March, Charlie Co., and Delta Co. as well, had suffered casualties at least equal to ours and had no personnel to give to us. We were assigned as the recon squad for Gardez, so we were already the most diminutive single unit on the firebase. After losing Browning and SFC Holliday, we had to operate a man down on each team. Our first battalion mission after their loss had 2nd Platoon Charlie Co., the two diminished Delta Co. sections, and our squad as part of a larger regional mission to track movement in the Paktia Province, the region in which Gardez is the capital of. Second Platoon Charlie Co., would be broken into three squads and was to perform roaming patrols in a specific pass that linked the Paktia Province to neighboring regions suspected of aiding enemy combatants.

It was a giant canyon, a half a mile deep and three miles long. Water must have run through the bottom where thousands of years ago forces beyond my comprehension divided the earth apart. The canyon was rocky, but otherwise barren and ran almost straight down from the top for almost three miles. There was some sporadically placed juniper green foliage along the canyon walls, and the bottom ran dry, which allowed for trails and easy transport. It also provided perfect cover for enemy fortifications.

For the mission, two squads would be on constant patrol, with the third down and resting. Every four hours the squads would rotate, so they patrolled for eight and rested for four, and this was to continue for four straight days. Lt. Youngblood and his two Delta trucks would provide mounted troop support for the rotating Charlie squads. Our squad was to be split into fire teams, and without detection, follow the basic route of the roaming Charlie squads from the top of the valley. Since we had just two fire teams to track two roaming squads, he didn't get any rest. They told us not to worry, that it'd be only four days and that we'd get a couple of hours here and there to rest. We didn't get to sleep, but at least we weren't bait, like the line boys. The idea was that the constant activity of the soldiers at the bottom of the canyon for four straight days would have to draw the attention of Taliban fortifications within the area. It was thought that the Taliban would likely not fire upon the troops if they were to spot them, out of fear that they might call more military attention to the area. This was the theory after a number of American units were attacked shortly after coming out of the canyon.

Most of the units were attacked a couple of hours later from the rear of their formations. It was thought that the attacked units must have been spotted by an enemy element that let them pass through the area first. They must have then followed them out to attack them away from their areas of operation. As the recon element, our job was to scale the top of the canyon along the edge, the whole time observing the goings on below and within the canyon walls. Our troops would not be likely to arouse gun fire, but they would no doubt, in the four days, force the Taliban fighters out of their caves for observation. When they came out, we would hold our fire as well, we were to record the exact grid coordinance of the activity and continue our reconnaissance without detection. The idea was that they'd be busy the whole time watching Charlie and Delta, while we watched them. Charlie Co. was to move out by Blackhawk on the fourth night just beyond the canyon's end.

During the first two days, Charlie Co. didn't run any patrols for three hours at a time, giving us enough time to catch a couple hours sleep. The third night saw an increase in activity, which led to more activity the next day, and an eventual extension to our mission. None of the Charlie Co. patrols had drawn any gunfire, a few soldiers observed movement coming from caves along the canyon walls, but none reacted hastily. Neither side had fired a shot the whole mission, which was seen as a great success. Without bringing attention to our location, we observed over twenty enemy fortifications along the canyon walls, which was why we were told by battalion to perform an additional night of observation, and that Charlie Co. would be extracted the following morning at 0430, just before daybreak.

None of us had slept in two days, and our

sustainment was no longer a question of mind over matter. Everybody was mentally and physically exhausted. For four days, and with a total of maybe six hours sleep, we had been on constant patrol. The whole time avoiding detection while leaning over rock faces, staring a half a mile down at a demise that could come far too easily by the mere slip of a rock, or a busted branch. None of us had anything left. Sgt. Lyons insisted that we maintain through the morning. But after a quiet meeting between him, Sgt. Eden, and SSG Reynolds, it was agreed that we would split the squad into three separate elements. Dorn and Ant would be taken from Alpha and Bravo respectively and link up with SSG Reynolds to form a third recon patrol. The meeting heard some of the only spoken words of the entire four and a half days. Our noise and light discipline was such that we were told that we were not to verbally communicate at all, unless shots were fired. Everything for four days was by hand signals. I heard Sgt. Eden and Sgt. Lyons give a few commands, but other than that, I didn't hear a word spoken until SSG Reynolds told us we had another day.

Sgt. Eden and I patrolled the last element before the extraction was to take place at 0430. It began at 0100 that morning. We walked together along the edge of the canyon. I looked down only about every tenth step. As I looked back fifty feet or so at Sgt. Eden, it was clear that he wasn't taking it so lightly. Through the light of the nearly full moon, I could see him with his map in hand. Every few minutes he would stop and record a grid coordinant or whatever else in a little green tablet that he carried with him on every patrol, no matter how routine. The moonlight was of a different kind that night. It was clear out, and the moon was nearly full, so visibility was ideal, which just meant that we had to be all the more careful not to be spotted. It was the bluish hue of the night that I remember best. Of how the rock was cleaner than it was in other areas I had seen. It was a cool gray instead of the dusty brown of most places. It wasn't covered in layers of sand and dirt, browned with the earthy colors of the terrain around it. Maybe it was the way the wind came through the pass that kept the rocks cleaner and sleeker than anywhere else. I remember that bluish haze and how it distracted me, of how my toppling body brought me back to the reality of situation.

It was straight down from the top, but in some areas it was straighter down than in others. Where I hung was straight-fucking-down. I remember, because when I looked down all I saw was myself suspended in a void of air from the waste down. I was just walking along and lost my footing. I felt my foot slide out with some loose soil. It slid to the outside as it came down to the ground. I felt the slip, it was slow, and I didn't think much of it. By the time I reached the point where my reflexes told me that my foot wasn't going to catch, I was down, and hanging from a protruding rock edge by the death grip I had on a small tree. My reaction was to kick my legs around, but I knew there was nothing there, and that I would only further stress the already shallow and weak roots of the foot tall baby tree that was currently saving my life. My rifle hung from its sling across my chest. I had both hands grasped around the thin trunk. I was panicked, but not enough to call for Sgt. Eden. I didn't want to break noise and light discipline. I'd never been a betting man, and haven't become one sense, but I pulled on that little tree and tested its strength to its very limits. In the meantime, Sgt. Eden must have noticed that I was not ahead of him. A wave of relief came over me as saw him coming. I called out in a whisper, "Sgt. Eden, here, help me."

He heard me the first time and I didn't have to call out again. He closed the gap between us quickly. He dropped and slid on his knees as he came to me. He ripped his sling from his body, and set his weapon to the side, he reached and grabbed me by the vest with both hands, "I got you Harris, I got you man, I got you," and with everything he had, he jerked me up the ledge. As he pulled me up, the two of us fell back. With our feet still at the edge, we laid there for a moment. Sgt. Eden was more shaken up than I was. He got up first. He reached down and pulled and dragged me off about ten feet back from the rocky edge, it was then that I first noticed that I had pissed myself. Sgt. Eden collapsed down next to me again and his hand flopped over and fell on my chest. I grabbed it with mine and with us both flat on our backs, holding each other's hands, maintaining noise and light discipline, he whispered, "Fuck you man."

WAR ZONE NUDIE BOOTH

I didn't land a guard shift. We had no patrols the next day, and we were to leave Firebase Gardez in less than a week. Some of the guys from Charlie Co. finessed one of the interpreters into getting them some bottles of whiskey. Since the towers were the only safe place from the intrusions of staff sergeants and above, guard shifts were a hot commodity that night. On that late winter eve, tower 1 and 2 of Firebase Gardez were the only venues for the hottest invitation only party in town. I wasn't on the guest list. Catching wind of the planned goings on of the evening, but not receiving an invitation, made me feel like I was in high school again. I was about to graduate, but with no beer bash awaiting my arrival.

The events that transpired during my day shift were, dare I say, bitter sweet. What would later happen would be the most detestable occurrence that I witnessed in a long list of abhorrent incidents. I hated that this thing would be the most vivid and lasting memory I had from the war. And I hated myself for even seeing it.

From 1400 to 1600 hours, Doc Evans and I were scheduled for occupancy of tower 2. I was put off at first about spending my last shift there. I preferred the scenic view of the Hindu Kush to the threatening hue of the city. But at least I was with Doc, who I could count on to say nothing unless I initiated the conversation, which I didn't plan to do. Not that I didn't like Doc, I just wanted to spend some of my last moments in Gardez in silent reflection. Climbing up that wooden ladder for the last time, I realized halfway up that my two hours would be spent in complete anxious tension. I replayed in my head the scene of Sgt. Lyons being sent back down to the earth after the RPG explosion killed Browning and Showalter up top. It was hard to stand for two hours in the exact spot that my best friend was killed. The smell was out of the tower by then, but the memory of the incident brought it frighteningly back every time I stepped in. That hot chalky smell of smoke and a stench of iron and blood filled my nostrils as I looked out upon the city. I would have asked Doc if he smelled anything, but I knew he didn't, I knew it was only me. The only way to get rid of that smell was to not go in tower 2 of Firebase Gardez, and in a few more days, I wouldn't have to.

Shortly after Browning and Showalter were killed, in addition to the refortification that took place, a spotting scope was put up to enable us to more efficiently survey the area. I enjoyed the magnified view for a few minutes without any intention of searching for hostile activity. I was occupied with observing a group of small children playing halfway between us and the city. As I watched them, I could see that they were walking toward us, and I thought about when Valentine and I watched the farm boy from tower 1, and what had happened to him.

Looking closer, I could see that there was nothing to be particularly concerned about this group, which consisted of four girls, none older than fourteen. A couple of minutes went by as I watched these four young girls through the scope, their faces becoming clearer with every step toward me. It was my dwelling on the tranquility that the whole scene brought me that kept me distracted by the suspicious nature of the circumstances. It was to say the least, calming to watch these girls merrily walking, completely uninhibited by the harsh realities of their surroundings. I was leaving in just a day, but I wanted to forget where I was right then. I will always remember their faces, and how they made that possible, if only for an hour.

When they got close enough for Doc Evans to see clearly with his naked eye, he asked me, "Hey Harris, swing that scope over there towards those four people, see what the fuck they're doing over there, they've been walking in this direction for a few minutes now." I moved the scope around a bit so as to make Doc think I had to redirect the scope to see them.

"Those four over there?"

"Yeah, I think they walked from the city, but I don't know for sure. You see anything?" I knew they had no weapons, I knew that they were just kids, and I knew that they were all girls. I could have described to him the subtle differences in shade of their angelic brown eyes. "Uhhh, let's see, no dude, I think… yeah, they're all girls."

"Well yeah, but that doesn't mean shit. Fuck, that kid that stuck Simeon with that knife downtown was a little girl, no older than nine."

"Yeah, I know, but they don't have shit, they're just playing." My tone shortened, Doc's suspicion angered me. These four girls were giving me the best semblance of humanity that I'd gotten in months.

"Alright, well, just keep an eye on 'em man. I mean I don't know why they're walking over here."

"How about you keep a fucking eye on them if you're so fucking suspicious Doc. Don't be telling me what the fuck is up, giving me tasks. I don't take orders from POGs Doc, so just watch your lane, roger?" I knew halfway through that what I was saying was unwarranted. Doc never flexed nuts, and wasn't trying to here.

"Chill out Harris, I ain't trying to give you orders man, come on." I didn't say anything back. I stepped to the side and waved my hand sarcastically at the scope, inviting him to take over if he so pleased.

"Go ahead man, stay right on them if you like." Doc Evans stepped up to it in an appeasing gesture. "Go ahead, you got this, I'll just stand here and smoke for the next hour man." He didn't say anything, and I knew he wouldn't for the rest of the shift.

Two cigarettes later, and the girls began moving into

a kind of formation. I looked over at Doc who was still eyeing them through the spotting scope. His expression didn't change as he looked at them, and I wondered if his suspicions would be aroused by their movements. As I took another drag from my cigarette without results, I noticed that I had smoked the cherry all the way down to the filter and it had fallen off. I looked down between my feet and watched the cherry burn itself out on top of the compacted sandbags. I pulled my pack out from my left cargo pocket and lit another. The girls were standing in a straight line on top of a small berm, they stood as close to the fence as possible without having it at all block our view of them, maybe twenty feet back or so.

The tallest one, who didn't necessarily look like the oldest, put both hands straight up in the air, and began to wave them back and forth. "Doc, what's she doing man, she trying to get our attention?" He was still fixed on them.

"Yeah, I don't know man. Fuck, what the hell is this, what the fuck does she want?" I thought about the kid, he didn't have a weapon. He just waved over to us. Then he ended up being slaughtered by our guys. "She's just playing around, she's probably just waving to us. It's nothing. I stepped up to the window opening and stretched my body as far out as I could, and waved a single hand back and forth in the air, just a wave hello. As soon as began to wave, the same tall girl stopped waving her arms in the air and began to make a curious gesture, putting her hand straight down and then up to her face slowly, and repeated it over and over.

"What's she doing Doc?"

"She's motioning like she's eating, I think. Yeah, she's pretending to eat."

"She wants food. They're just hungry, they want food from us."

"Well we can't get them food."

"What the fuck do you mean Doc, they're fucking kids, why not? A box of MRE's? We've got hundreds." Doc's face was doing something that told me that he was pondering if this act would count as aiding our enemy.

"You can't here though Harris. We don't even have anything."

"Yeah no shit man. After the shift, though. I'll just grab a box of MRE's and toss it over the hescos to them, they're four fucking kids Doc, they don't have weapons, they're fucking girls, they're like twelve years old for fuck sake. You're getting paranoid man."

"I'm just saying Harris, we can't just go throwing our MREs over the fence, for some Afghani kids, they bitched at us for giving them the candy out of our MREs during patrols and shit. There's no fucking way dude."

"So, I'm not going to tell anyone. It's not like the fucking MREs are guarded or anything, nobody has to know Doc. Okay? Got me, Doc?"

"Do whatever you want Harris, I'm not covering your ass though if something happens."

"What the fuck is going to happen. What the fuck do you think will happen? I'm giving some kids some fucking food, we have plenty." This was as aggressively as I had ever spoken to Doc, or anybody in the squad for that matter.

"Whatever Harris, do what you want man. Just wait till the shift is done, okay."

"No, I'm gonna just leave right now. Just shut the fuck up, Doc." Both of our attentions had been diverted away from the kids. I was more worked up than Doc, he immediately went right back to them and said, "Holy fuck Harris, look at this shit." My head snapped over to the berm where they stood, and they were all three still in a line, nude as the day they were born.

"What the fuck are they doing?" Doc said nothing, I didn't look over at him, my eyes couldn't move from what I was seeing. "Why the fuck did they take their fucking clothes off, what the fuck man? What the fuck are they doing?" Doc said nothing. The girls spread out from one another. Staying in a line, they began to make sexually suggestive poses and gestures. Doc turned away from the scope and said to me, "They're putting on a show for us."

The girl on the far left couldn't have been older than twelve, her breasts hadn't even begun to develop. She was like a little boy still. I could see that she had no pubic hair as she stood with her legs twice shoulder width apart, her hands on her hips. The next girl was maybe her same age, stood the same way, but with her backside towards us. The next girl stood with her legs together, facing away from us, but bent over with her adolescent ass and genitalia showing from behind. The last girl, the tall one, was old enough to have breasts and was holding one in each hand, lifting one up slightly higher, than the other. The motions of their gestures stayed relatively the same, as if the whole routine were regularly choreographed. "Why the fuck are they doing this? Doc, what the fuck is going on?"

"Fuck man, I don't know. This is fucked up. You still gonna give 'em MREs?" I didn't answer right away, not because I had to think whether or not I was, but because I realized that they were counting on those MRE's. That's what they were motioning about, that was the signal. That's what this whole show was about. When I waved back at them, it meant to start up. Without my knowing it, we had made a deal with those four little girls, what we were seeing, was them doing their part. There before me were four pre-pubescent third world girls, putting on a show that would put most bachelor parties to shame; instead of dollar bills, they did it for packaged meals. I had never felt so detestable in my life, and I haven't since. I began to make desperate motions for them to stop, and to put their clothes back on. I motioned down with both of my hands, and all four girls laid on their backs and spread their legs open towards us. I stood in the window and took my vest off, then slowly put it back on again, trying to signal them in any way I could to stop what they were doing. Nothing worked, the more I signaled to them, regardless of the gestures, the more they tried to entertain. Doc said very little, he just stepped back away from the scope and went all the way to the back of the tower, where he could not see them down below. I watched them, not their bodies. I didn't want to look at all, but I couldn't look away from their blank little faces and stiff lifeless eyes. I knew that what I saw could not be put into reason. That hellish scene would be forever burned into the recesses of my mind. I looked away and smoked four cigarettes in a row until our shift had ended. Neither of us spoke or looked out the tower, we could have been attacked in those moments and would have never known. Dorn and Ant were to relieve us and yelled up at us about three minutes after our shift was over. We didn't even notice they were late.

"Yo Harris, it's Dorn. One of you come on down, we got this shit." Doc's face was blank and pale, he didn't make a move. I said to him, "Go ahead man, you go." I didn't expect to hear anything back.

"Hey man, I'll go get that box of MREs, I got it man."

"I got it Doc it's all good."

"No Harris, just let me man, I got it."

"Alright, thanks man." Doc fastened the chin strap on his helmet and began down the ladder. They put their clothes back on. The tallest one, already dressed, was making the eating motion with her hand again. I wanted her to know that I saw her, and that I would follow my end through. I stuck my hands straight up and out of the window, and gave her two thumbs up. I didn't know what else to do.

The girls started closer to the fence when Dorn was just getting to the top of the ladder. "Ant's taking a shit man, he'll be here soon. You can go down now if you like." I wouldn't have mentioned the girls, but they were coming right up to the hescos now, and at any minute, I knew that Doc could be seen throwing a box of MREs over, which I knew that Dorn would make a stink over.

"Hey man, there's like four girls fucking around close to the hescos. They've been here since we started our shift, they're just playing around and stuff, it's all good, they're not doing shit." As soon as four girls left my mouth, Dorn's brow popped up with excitement and a thrilled look took over both eyes.

"Hell yeah, they get naked for you?" Dorn stepped past me and to the window, sticking his body as far out as he could. What the fuck they doing by the hescos, you give 'em any MREs yet?" I looked out over Dorn's shoulder and I wanted to throw his leaning body from the top. The girls were standing patiently, and I could see Doc, carrying four boxes of MREs by their plastic straps, two in each hand. Dorn looked at me, then back out the window and shouted out at Doc. "What the fuck are you doing?" Doc, looked up and kept walking, then threw the MRE boxes over the hescos one by one, Dorn yelled again. "WHAT THE FUCK YOU DOING DOC?" When he looked back at me, I threw my fist at the side of his turning face with all the manifested hatred of the last four months. My right hook landed square on the left side of his face, I could feel the knuckle of my index finger against his moist eyeball. From the moment I made contact with his face from the time I watched him go spinning to the sandbagged floor, I had time to imagine how many guard shifts he had watched these same four girls go through their routine. Over the noise of Dorn's semi unconscious body slamming against the side of the tower, I didn't hear Ant coming up the ladder. Without hesitation, I followed Dorn to the ground, planting a knee on each side of his hips, I slammed my ass down on his stomach. I grasped the inside of his vest with my left hand I pumped my right hand back and forth as hard and as quickly as I could. Every time my fist slammed against his head, I mustered more strength and hatred for the next strike.

I must have hit him at least six times by the time Ant got to the top. He yelled out, "WHAT THE FUCK?" Ant pulled me off of Dorn and threw me against the side of the opposite wall. He hooked me in the side of the head with the force of a mule. Even with my helmet on, he knocked me as unconscious as Dorn. A few seconds later, when I got my wits about me, I was laying on the ground and watching Ant bent over on a knee next to Dorn, holding his bleeding head up with his hands. Ant heard me coming to and whipped his body around toward me, ready as if I were coming with a counter attack.

Still on the ground, I put both my hands up, shook my head back and forth and asked, "Is he alright?"

"What in the fuck is going on here, Harris? What the fuck happened?" Ant's body was turned toward Dorn, and he was still down on a knee, but his head was turned toward me. I could see Dorn coming to and just as I was about to say something, I don't know what, from laying flat on his side, Dorn popped up on his hands and knees and quickly said, "It's nothing, just talking shit. Just shit between me and Harris." Ant looked to Dorn, while Dorn's eyes were fixed on mine.

Ant turned his head back toward me and said, "Get the fuck out of here Harris, your shift is over. I got this." I got up on my hands and knees, then stood up slowly, the whole time my eyes stayed locked on Dorn's. As I went down the ladder I heard Dorn from up top, "This is our thing Harris, ain't no need to get Sgt. Eden involved. Hooah?"

After seeing what I had seen, and not being able to forget it then, or even now, I walked back to our tent with no intention of sharing the experience, or sharing what I had done to Dorn. The tent looked different than it did when I left for guard two hours earlier. The entirety of everybody's possessions was gathered on top of their respective bunks, which were in neat rows outside the tent. The two plus inches of dust accumulated on the floor, and anything that had not been touched in the last three days, was gone. The chalky haze was still in the air from when SSG Reynolds had swept and dusted just minutes before, such a housekeeper. When I walked in, the tent was empty except for him proudly standing in the middle, leaned against his broom with a look of satisfaction that I had not seen him wear in months. I couldn't make out Sgt. Lyons's shouts, but I knew immediately that the rest of the squad's whereabouts could be traced to that vicious shriek.

As I walked in SSG Reynolds said, "Harris?"

I acknowledged, "Just got off guard. Where's the rest of the squad?" I already knew that they were out back behind the tent getting torn into by Sgt. Lyons, what I meant was why. As the words left my mouth, both our attentions were turned toward the scream of Sgt. Lyon's yelling "FLUTTER KICKS, GO." SSG Reynolds chuckled casually as he leaned forward on his broom. "I don't think you want to go back there." I looked away from SSG Reynolds and toward the rear exit of the tent.

"You seen Doc Sergeant?"

"Yeah he came in here waiting for you I think," he pointed behind with his thumb. "He's with the rest of them now. I'd find somewhere else to be if I were you, Harris." I sighed slowly and walked past SSG Reynolds. I took off my vest and helmet and put it down next to the empty spot where my cot was. "Outside, Harris." I looked back at SSG Reynolds, nodded once with a crack of a smile and picked my stuff up and started toward the rear exit where I could hear Sgt. Lyons' screams getting louder. "Harris, not that way. Where the fuck you going?"

Without turning around I answered, "Nowhere else to go now, with the squad I guess Sergeant."

LAST CALL

The thing with Dorn made less of a stir than I had thought it would. Less than I wanted really. I'd been fighting an obscure adversary for the last three months. I wanted a face to face battle. And I hated Dorn. I knew that. Nobody really gave a shit though. Everyone inquired. But nobody cared. Sgt. Eden made us talk it out with one another. I had pretty much gotten what I wanted. I got to hit him in the face. And he didn't really want to get into the whole reason it went down, seeing how it would have made him look like a sick fucking pedophile and all. Everybody knew we had a long going beef, and Dorn didn't have enough rank for it to really matter, so the whole thing was swept under the rug very neatly. Out of respect for Sgt. Eden and his leadership, nobody really talked about the incident. Nobody wanted to imply that Sgt. Eden didn't have control of his guys. All that anybody really knew was that I had fucked Dorn up for some reason or the other. And that was all I really needed. Looking back, it was probably the only decent thing I did in Gardez. At the time though, it only increased the distance between me and everybody else.

"Hello?"

"It's me." What seemed like a minute of silence went by before I heard her voice again. I hadn't talked to her since I had yelled at her a month before. I didn't want to have to call, but I had nobody else to talk to. I knew that she would still be there.

"How are you?"

"I'm okay." I could hear her breath rush in to her mouth and stop, she held it in, then released it with a slow sigh.

"I'm glad."

"You're glad?"

"Mmhmm."

"Are you okay?"

"I'm great." Her sentences were short, and her words abrupt. Her voice stayed soft because it had no other to be.

"So I'm not supposed to tell you this…"

"Then don't."

"Well no, I mean, it's fine. I'm, well, we're all leaving in four days."

"You guys are coming home?" Her voice was the same, but her speech quickened.

"No, no, I'm sorry. I mean we're just leaving where we're at right now. We're just going back to Kandahar to refit. Then we're going to another firebase."

"For how long?"

"It should just be a couple more months.   Then we'll come home."

"Why can't you tell me that?"

"I don't know, COMSEC, you know."

"No, I don't. COMSED?"

"COMSEC, communication security, it's just like the stuff they tell you you're not suppose to say on the phone or in letters and stuff."

"Okay. Whatever. Well that will be good, right? You have been there almost four months straight, it'll be nice to see something new won't it?" The excitement that wanted to come through had dried up with her last sentence.

"Yeah, I mean, we all know the area now and stuff, but yeah, we need to get out of this place. It's been way too long. Too much shit's gone down here."

There was a long pause before she said anything, I didn't care, I liked just listening to her breathe. "I saw on the news about Browning, I'm so sorry baby."

"Yeah, it's uhhh, I don't know. That happened a while back now."

"Are you okay?"

"I'm fine. Yeah. Fine."

"I really miss you, baby."

"I miss you, too."

"You haven't called in a while. I was really worried."

"Yeah.   I'm   sorry,   I've   been...busy,   I'm   fine

though." For a few sentences, Samantha's voice had forgotten how I had talked to her last time on the phone. "I've just been so worried about you. And you were just so mean the last time we talked. You've never been like that to me. I just want you home so bad."

"I'm sorry about that. I don't know. It's just hard sometimes. I don't know how to be over here."

"But baby, it's me. You know how to be with me, I love you."

"I know, and I love you. I'm just losing my mind over here sometimes, not now though, I'm fine, it's usually fine. Just sometimes, it gets crazy. I don't know. I love you though babe. I just want to be with you again. I want to be home."

"Just don't be mean to me. You don't have to be happy, or in a good mood. You don't even have to be excited when I answer. I know how hard it must be. Just don't be mean to me, ever. And remember how much I love you. Don't forget about things here, you still have a life here with me, and I love that life. I just need to know that you still love it too." Her voice had cleared from the threat of oncoming tears and it was soft again like I always thought of it as being.

"I do babe, I still love you. I love you more than anything. I think about you all the time, all day. I can't wait till we can be together again. I just need to get home. Then everything will be fine. Things will be good. I just need to get through the next few months and we'll be fine."

"We will. You just don't get yourself too stressed

out…"

"What, babe…babe, I can't hear you."

"Jbssp…drfp…yjllk..k….k…"

"Babe, hold on, you're breaking up. Just a minute let me move around." I started pacing around desperately on top of the roof. I could hear only consonants through the static. "Babe, can you hear… FUCK…FUCK…fucking signal…fucking bullshit…" The line went dead and the signal diminished to an abrasive dial tone. The lines shorted out. Communications at the base were down for a week. That was the last phone call I would make from Gardez.

THE GUILTY DEMISE OF FARID FEKARI

After losing Browning, my cigarette intake went up like a motherfucker. Everybody's did, even Lt. Youngblood who never smoked in his life before Gardez was taking them down like a cowboy. Sgt. Eden chewed and smoked now, always one or the other, and sometimes both. I was never a smoker, but was at a pack a day by then, and Farid was the man to go to for smokes. After three months in Gardez, the escalation of hostility was such that our patrols downtown and into the market areas slowed to a halt. Most of the villagers liked us in the beginning. The marketers saw us as a business opportunity, just as our bosses saw them. Our presence in and around Gardez had stirred increased Taliban resentment in the area. And as the majority of the cities populace was in the beginning sympathetic to American intentions, those same hostilities were as often directed toward the people of Gardez. By this time, it was no longer possible for us to go to the market for anything. Our visits either meant a direct attack by surveying Taliban forces, or the immediate execution of the marketer upon our departure. With fifty soldiers who needed cigarettes like they needed air, a man on the inside was a hot commodity. Farid was that man. He could get cigarettes two packs for a dollar, instead of the dollar they charged us. Farid would always front you if you needed him to. He had been burned a few times doing such favors. I think I still owe him about six dollars.

Farid was also the guy I talked to most. Valentine had shut down at this point. Shut it all out. He was the same soldier I suppose, he walked as tall, and he even kept smiling. He ran the SAW like he ran his life. Always reasoned, unwavering regardless of circumstance. But by this time he had only the energy to do his job and to love his wife. That's what it was for Valentine. He loved his wife like the purest of men do. He loved his wife in the way that Hector loved his. He loved being a paratrooper, and he loved to run SAW. But the love he had for his wife, and hers for him, was of a kind that every man who fought in this war needs to go home to for the hope that it will someday restore some of the humanity that we lost over there. He wrote all day. If he wasn't on patrol or guard, he wrote. Nobody had to ask what or who to. That's when he smiled, only when he would write. He would lay on his stomach across his cot with a legal pad and blue pen. If it were night he would write under the illumination of his head-lamp. I watched him at night when he wrote. I watched his expressions. I would look at his pen moving across the page, when it would pause for a moment, I looked up at him to find him more often than not with a Cupid struck grin across his broad face. We didn't talk anymore, but he couldn't help but still share that Valentine glow, even if it was only on occasion.

The bullshit sessions that were so plentiful in our early days at the firebase had completely dried up. Sgt. Eden was completely consumed by Gardez. When I think about it now, I understand better what made him increasingly disconnected. Sgt. Eden was terrified. Not of dying or being horribly wounded, I can't imagine those thoughts entered his mind. Sgt. Eden became increasingly aware that no matter what he did, he could lose one of us at any time. And the tension between Dorn and me had manifested into more violence, and despite the effective illusion, he knew that 'Alpha Team' was falling apart.

He mostly just read old operation orders and compared them with journal entries he had kept about every mission we did. He began to even record a kind of field inventory of vehicles and big rocks and such that were along our patrol routes. He would record drawings of various objects, perhaps a disabled roadside vehicle. He would specify the appearance of the object as it looked from a given angle. There were countless patrols where we would stop before coming up on something and he would pull out his notepad and study the object, comparing it to his technical drawing, if the object appeared any differently than how he recorded it, he assumed that the object had been tampered with and was likely an improvised explosive device. That's the kind of shit that kept Sgt. Eden occupied for almost every waking moment. That's the kind of shit that probably kept us alive in Gardez. Toward the end, I thought of it mostly as keeping him from being my friend.

By this time, Farid was my most likely companion in conversation, and I clung on to that human connection with little thought of what our relationship did for him. For everything that he did for me, I cannot remember him asking for more than an old used up porn mag, which I never did get to him. Farid enjoyed my company because I treated him slightly better than most of the soldiers of Gardez treated the interpreters, which is to say, that I had conversations with him that transcended favors and errands. We talked about religion, philosophy, and sex. I learned through Farid that there is, regardless of environment, some very base commonalities regarding humanistic inquiry and insecurities that are one hundred percent universal. Yet there was always a difference. I would always look upon Farid with different eyes. He felt that distance that I always put between us. And that's what I regret most about our friendship, that I never granted him the impartiality of our differences as he did for me.

I remember the last time I spoke to Farid very vividly. It was March 21, the spring equinox, and the day seemed ripe with revival. Since our arrival the hostilities of the weather had run a close second to those of the Taliban. The air was starting to make that turn that it does at the end of winter. There was no longer that cold sting in your lungs when you breathed in deeply. The air was ripe with the smells of flourishing vegetation. It was still cool, but when you stood in the sun, the warmth was enough to fill your cheek with that glorious feeling of being. We were to leave Gardez in just three days. By this time, our sins ran deeper than our mere occupation. We left a stench of wrongdoing that would taint the air for long after we were gone. I guess you couldn't say that while in Gardez we shat where we ate, because we didn't have to keep eating there. We shat where they ate, and then we just left.

Farid approached me on the first morning of spring in 2003. All we had were routine patrols for the three days we had left at Gardez, and everybody in the squad just slept all day, even Sgt. Eden and Sgt. Lyons. A part of me wished for a mission, I was glad to be leaving Gardez, but I knew that the show wasn't over, that I just had to switch venues. I still got up early every morning, just after the sun had come up to warm the cool ground of the valley floor. The morning prayers of the villagers could be heard in unison faintly from the firebase. By that time, I had them memorized. Farid was always up doing the prayers too, and I often met him at the piss tubes just as he was finishing up. Farid was curiously apprehensive that morning as he approached me.

Farid and I usually met at the tubes and we had enjoyed a piss together in which he would ignite the conversation with a wave from across the way and a good-humored, 'Harris, good morning my man. How are you today?' That morning, I had gotten to the tubes just before him. As I pissed, I saw him approach. He stopped short of the tubes and hung back. I figured he just didn't have to go, but wanted to say hi anyway. I finished and walked over to him where he was facing the guard tower with his back turned toward me. "Farid, what's up, man? It's finally fucking warming up." He stood with his back turned to me still, and without moving his feet, he twisted his body halfway around to face me as we spoke. I couldn't remember seeing his face so expressionless since the first time SFC Holliday brought him into our tent. "Farid, what's up man, you alright?"

"I am good, Harris. Are you good?"

"Yeah man, we're fucking outta here finally man, another unit's coming in." Farid turned back straight, so he was facing away from me again. Without thinking much of it at the time, I just stepped over a bit so we were face to face. He gave me a quaint look of disapproval as I repositioned myself, but he did not move his body or head away from me. "Yes. I heard. Lt. Youngblood said that the next unit wouldn't need our help. They got people from the US to come help you guys now. So I guess I'll be going back to live in the city."

"What do you mean, 10th Mountain isn't going to use you guys as their interpreters?"

"No, they have people coming from the US to speak Dari and Pashtun, they don't want to use us."

"What, are we doing that too, now? Don't the other firebases around here use you guys from the nearby villages too?"

"Yes, but no more. They want to contract."

"To contract? What do you mean they want to contract?"

"They have contracts, and they pay people in the US now to come here and interpret for you soldiers."

"What the fuck, why? Why don't they just use you guys? You guys know what's up around here, not just how to speak, you know the goddamn villagers. So now what, they're just going to have like recent college grads who studied the language come over here and do this shit?" Farid's face was no longer expressionless, he wore a tight lipped frown.

"They want Americans, no Afghanis."

"So, you're leaving the base then?"

"I will leave in three days, for good."

"With us?"

"Not with you, Harris. You will go to Orgun-E and then back to America. I will go back to the city."

"So this is happening now, with the new interpreters and shit. I wonder if we're going to have them at the new firebase?"

"Yes, Harris, you will. Lt. Youngblood said that all units will use the US interpreters."

"That's fucked up. It doesn't even make any sense. It's just going to cost them even more. They don't pay you guys shit. They're going to have to give these guys six figures, you fucking know it." My words fell light on Farid's ears. He knew I didn't really give a shit about him. I thought about what he meant to me. I didn't think about what not having us meant to Farid.

"Yes, it's fine. I'll find new job. Harris, that porn magazine, did you?"

"Oh man, yeah dude, fuck. I still need to grab that. I'll... fuck man, I would go get it now, but all the porn is in the squad box, and everybody's still asleep. You'll be around for a few more days though, right?"

"Yes. I'll be around, in two days. Then I leave."

"In two days, what do you mean? You're leaving, and coming back?"

"I'm going into the city this morning and will be back in two days. Then I leave again. I have to come back for my money. Then I'll go back."

"Why the fuck don't they just pay you now."

"They say they can't pay now, they haven't got my money."

"What the fuck is that?" Farid was talking to me more like he used to at this point.

He put his hands up in a passive gesture, answering, "I don't want to make trouble, so I'll just come back in two days."

"Why don't you just hang out until they have your money man, we're just running patrols. We'll be around pretty much all day."

"They need to take down our tent. Lt. Youngblood said that they need to build an ammo bunker where our tent is. So we're just going to leave now, instead of moving our tent for just two days."

"What the fuck, are you serious? What the fuck do

189

we need another ammo bunker for, that's bullshit?"

"We don't want to make any trouble, Harris. You guys don't need us now, so we will leave. Be careful, Harris." Farid looked through my eyes for the longest second and walked off. It felt like I'd never see him again, and I had to follow him, "So that's just it man, I'm not going to see you again?"

"You see me in two days. I'll be back for my money, Harris."

"That's it though man?"

"Yes, Harris, unless you come back to Gardez some day." I saw only his back. As I talked and followed him, he just kept walking. "Hey man, well dude, I can get you that mag still. Goddamn man, I'm sorry. I can't believe I forgot that. When are you leaving today?"

"I leave now, Harris."

"Okay, well I can definitely get it for you when you come back." I watched his head nod up and down from behind. "Say man, you think you could pick me up like a carton of smokes? I can get you back when I give you the mag in a couple of days." He must have been astonished by my aloofness. I don't know for sure, because his face never said it.

He stopped suddenly to turn around and answered me, "Yes, Harris, I'll get you cigarettes. But I must go now. I'm leaving now, Harris." Without waiting for my response, he had already turned and started to walk away.

Two days passed and Farid never came to pick up his money. The other interpreters came back, but not Farid.

Lt. Youngblood showed no concern, and the squad pondered his whereabouts for about two minutes upon hearing the news during the nightly squad brief. We were leaving Gardez the next day, and nobody gave a shit anymore. Maybe we never did.

Most of the squad was either occupied with various reading materials, or the majority, playing poker at one of two card tables. SSG Reynolds controlled the game at one table, Valentine at the other. I was hanging on with half the chips I started with. I was playing at Reynolds' table. I wanted to be at the other table where Tolson was. Also Valentine was taking a break from his writing to share his merriment. The conversation at my table was well monopolized between Van Dorn's hunting stories, and him and Ant's compared football/fuck stories. Dorn's face was still a bit fucked up. It wasn't swollen anymore, and it wasn't black and blue, but his skin still had that yellow and purple hue that told the story. And he didn't have that date rapist look on his face when he looked at me anymore.

I didn't care much to break the monotony of the discourse because all of Ant's stories involved tight pussied teenagers, which was always good for squad morale. I thought of Farid. Not where he was or why he didn't come back for his money, although that was considerably troubling, I thought mostly about the lack of concern in the tent. I looked around at everybody at our table, then I looked over at the other table, I looked at Sgt. Eden and Doc Evans as they laid on their bunks reading. Farid was the last thought on anybody's mind, and I marveled at how that was. Farid had saved my life at least once. He had saved all of Alpha team's lives. For first squad, Farid was a part of Gardez, and we were leaving Gardez, so nobody gave a shit. He once told me that he only got paid twenty dollars a week to help us, but I knew that he needed that money. And mostly I hoped that he had wanted to say goodbye.

It happened maybe two hours after SSG Reynolds put out the squad briefing. Lt. Youngblood walked into the tent as he did ten times at day, "Sergeant Reynolds, can I get you a moment when you have a chance here?" He stepped right back outside, SSG Reynolds folded his hand and walked out. Just a couple of minutes later, Ant was right in the middle of telling about one of his many triumphs, when SSG Reynolds came back in the tent with Lt. Youngblood right behind him.

"Alright first squad, listen up. The Lieutenant and some of his boys just got back from a mounted patrol. They passed by the city on their way back and it looks like the Taliban are strong in the area right now. We're on high alert until we leave, we think they know that we're leaving tomorrow, and they want to hit us hard again before we go. Lt. Youngblood will give you the details." He turned back toward the Lieutenant, nodded slightly and gave him the floor, "Lieutenant."

"Thank you Sergeant. Okay first squad, first I just want to thank you for your time spent here in Gardez. Your squad was picked to run recon patrols at this post for good reason, you've faced a lot of adversary while here, and you've fought like paratroopers all the way through, Airborne." Everybody yelled back with an enthusiastic 'AIRBORNE'. I said nothing. "Anyway, like SSG Reynolds said, we have reason to believe that the Taliban's strength in the area has increased and that they are deliberately targeting this post, specifically, your squad before you leave. Now, you guys just heard in your squad brief about how Farid was supposed to come back today to pick up his money but never did; well, we found him propped up on the side of the road on our way back to the firebase just now." He paused for a moment to look across the expressionless faces. "We know it's got to be the Taliban, they were definitely trying to make an example."

I couldn't help myself, without thinking at all I stood up and blurted out, "What the fuck does that mean? Propped up? An example? Just what the FUCK does that mean, Lieutenant?" Sgt. Eden looked over at me, just like everybody else did, surprised. Sgt. Lyons snapped up and turned toward me, but then said nothing and looked at the Lieutenant, whose countenance remained unresponsive.

Without hesitation and with unblinking eyes Lt. Youngblood said to me, "His head was cut off and put on a steak. It was stuck in the middle of the road back to post. We stopped and secured the area, we did a search, but there was nothing, just his fucking head on a stick. It was definitely Farid." He looked away from me and panned across the rest of the tent with the words, "So watch out paratroopers, the enemy is out there."

That was it, the end of the meeting. The Lt. just

walked out.   And without additional words from SSG Reynolds, everybody went right back to their bullshit. Here's where I wish I had something better to write, maybe a poignant and poetic abstraction of a shared moment of rekindled humanity between the squad would be more inspiring, but that shit didn't happen.   Nobody gave a fuck. Nobody gave a fuck about the villagers.   Nobody gave a fuck about the farmers.   Nobody gave a fuck about the dying unarmed boy.   Nobody gave a fuck about the prepubescent girls they were jerking off to.   And nobody gave a fuck about Farid's head on a pike.   Nobody gave a fuck about Gardez.   All we gave a fuck about was leaving. And that's what we got.   As scheduled, we left the next day. The army gave us just what we needed, and nothing more. Just like Farid had said.

Reviews

Made in the USA
Las Vegas, NV
26 August 2022